Research Foundation Year in Review
2013

Statement of Purpose

The CFA Institute Research Foundation is a not-for-profit organization established to promote the development and dissemination of relevant research for investment practitioners worldwide.

Neither the Research Foundation, CFA Institute, nor the publication's editorial staff is responsible for facts and opinions presented in this publication. This publication reflects the views of the author(s) and does not represent the official views of the Research Foundation or CFA Institute.

The CFA Institute Research Foundation and the Research Foundation logo are trademarks owned by The CFA Institute Research Foundation. CFA®, Chartered Financial Analyst®, AIMR-PPS®, and GIPS® are just a few of the trademarks owned by CFA Institute. To view a list of CFA Institute trademarks and the Guide for the Use of CFA Institute Marks, please visit our website at www.cfainstitute.org.

© 2014 The CFA Institute Research Foundation

All rights reserved. No part of this publication may be reproduced, stored in a retrieval system, or transmitted, in any form or by any means, electronic, mechanical, photocopying, recording, or otherwise, without the prior written permission of the copyright holder.

This publication is designed to provide accurate and authoritative information in regard to the subject matter covered. It is sold with the understanding that the publisher is not engaged in rendering legal, accounting, or other professional service. If legal advice or other expert assistance is required, the services of a competent professional should be sought.

ISBN 978-1-934667-67-5

7 March 2014

Editorial Staff

Maryann Dupes
Book Editor

Abby Farson Pratt
Assistant Editor

Mike Dean
Publishing Technology Specialist

Cindy Maisannes
Manager, Publications Production

Christina Hampton
Publishing Technology Specialist

Randy Carila
Publishing Technology Specialist

Contents

I. The Year in Review
Message from the Chair.. 1
Executive Director's Report 3
Research Director's Report 5

II. Monograph Summaries
Life Annuities: An Optimal Product for Retirement Income............. 11
    by Moshe A. Milevsky
Fundamentals of Futures and Options.. 15
    by Roger G. Clarke, Harindra de Silva, CFA,
        and Steven Thorley, CFA
Manager Selection 25
    by Scott D. Stewart, CFA

III. Literature Review Summaries
Ethics and Financial Markets: The Role of the Analyst 29
    by Marianne M. Jennings
The Evolution of Asset/Liability Management................................ 37
    by Ronald J. Ryan, CFA

IV. Multimedia Summaries
Fund Management: An Emotional Finance Perspective (audio book)   45
    by David Tuckett and Richard J. Taffler
"The Great Confusion: Reflections on Mean–Variance
    Optimization" with Harry Markowitz (webinar)......................... 49
    by Nathan Erickson, CFA

V. Workshop for the Practitioner Summaries
"Who Should Hedge Tail Risk?" Presented by Robert Litterman 51
    by Bud Haslett, CFA, and Laurence B. Siegel
Specifying and Managing Tail Risk in Multi-Asset Portfolios 55
    by Pranay Gupta, CFA

VI. James R. Vertin Award
James R. Vertin Award.. 61
Evolving into the Science of Investing: Presentation upon
    Receiving the James R. Vertin Award 63
    by Ronald N. Kahn
Observations from a Career in Investment Management:
    Presentation upon Receiving the James R. Vertin Award............. 71
    by Richard Grinold

VII. Research Foundation Leadership Circle 75

VIII. Recent Publications from the Research Foundation Archive 77

Message from the Chair

As chair of the CFA Institute Research Foundation's Board of Trustees, I would like to thank you for your interest in and support of the Research Foundation. It is because of you that we are able to advance the understanding of investment markets.

Established in 1965 and endowed by generous contributions from a number of prominent investment professionals and organizations, the CFA Institute Research Foundation is governed by an all-volunteer board of trustees and supported by a small staff. Our mission is to provide in-depth, high-quality investment research to the global investment community. This worldwide audience reflects the diversity of the modern investment industry—security analysts, portfolio managers, traders, brokers, consultants, fund sponsors (staff as well as trustees), and academics. It includes CFA Institute members and non-members alike.

To address the needs of such a broad audience, Research Foundation authors are practitioners and academics who are committed to producing investment research that is oriented to the practical application of investment finance. The research topics cover all fields relevant to investment professionals, and although that coverage may involve topical investment issues, the Research Foundation's research is meant to distinguish itself not by its timeliness but rather its timelessness.

The majority of our research is published in book form, but we also produce literature reviews, webinars, occasional papers, and seminars on investment issues of particular interest. Notably, the Research Foundation hosts a workshop that is held just prior to the start of the CFA Institute Annual Conference. All Research Foundation materials are distributed online for free, with the hardcopy version offered at a low price.

I hope you enjoy this issue of the *Research Foundation Year in Review*. I urge you to explore the impressive body of research that the Research Foundation has produced over the years. We welcome your comments and suggestions on how best to expand and distribute that work.

Jeffery V. Bailey, CFA
Chair
The CFA Institute Research Foundation

Executive Director's Report

Welcome to the 2013 edition of the *Research Foundation Year in Review*. We are delighted to share with you the high-quality, practitioner-focused research that you have come to expect during our 48-year history. In 2013, we produced books and literature reviews on the topics of ethics, asset/liability management, derivatives, life annuities, and manager selection. These works will be reviewed further in the Research Director's Report.

Looking Back: 2013

Many Research Foundation (RF) firsts took place in 2013, such as the first Asia-Pacific hosting of the Research Foundation Workshop for the Practitioner. This Singapore-based event featured RF board member Pranay Gupta, CFA, and Robert B. Litterman discussing the intricacies of managing tail risk. The year also featured a new RF Twitter account (@CFAResearchFndn), from which we shared highlights of our content with more than 7,000 followers—all in 140 characters or fewer. If you are not doing so already, we sincerely hope you will take a few minutes to read the tweets and become some of our newest followers:

The RF's work with member societies continued in 2013. The CFA Society Toronto and CFA Society San Francisco each hosted one of the semiannual RF board meetings. The Toronto event featured the Vertin Awards, where active investing luminaries Grinold and Kahn received their well-deserved accolades. The Research Foundation Society Award was also granted for the second year. Our congratulations go out to the following winning societies for their excellent work in using RF content in their events and activities:

- CFA Society Barbados
- CFA Society Hawaii
- CFA Society Pakistan
- CFA Society Italy
- CFA Society Emirates
- CFA Society Toronto
- CFA Society France (Encouragement Award)

Research Foundation Year in Review 2013

The RF was pleased to have content highlighted by CFA Institute's Future of Finance program during 2013, and we look forward to contributing additional content in 2014. The RF was also delighted to have contributed content for use in the CIPM curriculum. We hope to assist in the future by providing curriculum content for other efforts, including the CFA Program.

Finally, 2013 was significant for another reason: It marks the last year of operations as the Research Foundation of CFA Institute. Beginning in January 2014, we will become the CFA Institute Research Foundation. You can rest assured that even with a new name and logo, we will continue to produce the same high-quality, relevant investment content that you have come to expect.

Please join me in thanking CFA Institute, the RF Board of Trustees, and the societies, donors, authors, volunteers, universities, and others who help make the Research Foundation the great organization that it is.

Bud Haslett, CFA
Executive Director
The CFA Institute Research Foundation

Research Director's Report

In 2013, authors chosen and financially supported by the Research Foundation produced three monographs and two literature reviews for the community of investment practitioners.

Monographs

Moshe A. Milevsky, *Life Annuities: An Optimal Product for Retirement Income*. In *Life Annuities*, York University (Toronto, Canada) Professor Moshe Milevsky provides great detail on the different types of life annuities offered by the insurance industry and on how the prices for these financial instruments are determined. Life annuities are widely regarded as a good solution to the problem, faced by those saving for retirement, of spreading the income from an individual's working life over his or her whole life. By pooling the mortality risk of a large number of annuitants, an insurance company can (while making a profit) provide the annuitants with a much larger income, during the time they are alive, than they could provide for themselves if they had to make their savings last to the outer limit of their possible life span, say, age 107.

Because the debate on the proper role of annuities has heated up recently, it is important to know the basics about this product. Milevsky clears up many misunderstandings about annuities and emphasizes that *life annuities*, which are designed to solve the mortality-risk problem just described, are a small subset of the much larger umbrella category of *annuities*, most of which have little in common with life annuities.

The book is organized into four large sections: (1) institutional details, (2) 10 formulas to know, (3) the scholarly literature, and (4) conclusions and final thoughts. A question-and-answer format is used in the first two sections.

Institutional details include the exact nature of a life-annuity contract, the differences among types of annuities, and "riders" or options attached to life annuities that attempt to make them more attractive to investors. This section also addresses credit risk (the risk that the benefit will not be paid), the size of the life-annuity market, the names and characteristics of leading issuers, taxation of annuities, guarantees of annuity benefits by state-organized funds in the United States, and the cost to the investor of typical annuities.

The second section covers annuity pricing. The basic formula for pricing a life insurance or annuity contract was discovered by the British mathematician Benjamin Gompertz in 1825. In this section, Milevsky draws the reader through a series of formulae and examples designed to make annuity pricing clear and simple.

The third section describes the existing literature on annuities, much of which is devoted to the "annuity puzzle"—the question of why annuities are not more widely held. The author reviews the broad literature on life-cycle consumption and investing, the impact of annuities on pension and retirement policy, and the role of annuities in personal financial planning.

One important decision is *when* to annuitize. A currently popular idea is that it is better to wait until old age to annuitize part or all of one's wealth. Milevsky suggests that this advice is flawed. The final section presents the author's conclusions.

Roger G. Clarke, Harindra de Silva, CFA, and Steven Thorley, CFA, *Fundamentals of Futures and Options.* Roger Clarke of Ensign Peak Advisors, Harindra de Silva, CFA, of Analytic Investors, and Steven Thorley, CFA, of Brigham Young University provide readers with tools for understanding the two basic types of financial derivatives: (1) futures, which enable a buyer to pay now (at a price agreed upon now) for the future delivery of some good or service, and (2) options, which convey to the holder the right but not the obligation to engage in some specified transaction. Most derivatives are built out of these elemental parts, so understanding futures and options is critical to a broader understanding of derivatives and of financial markets generally. (Note that this monograph is an update of the 1992 book by Clarke: *Options and Futures: A Tutorial.*)

Options and futures prices are set in the market according to a number of arbitrage conditions, including put–call parity, spot–futures parity, and the Black–Scholes option pricing formula.

The Black–Scholes formula demonstrates that the fair or correct price of an option depends on the price of the underlying security, the strike price of the option, the volatility of the underlying security, the level of interest rates, and the option's time to expiration.

Although options and futures markets have sometimes been criticized as enabling investors to speculate and use leverage, the authors emphasize the role of derivatives in hedging, or risk reduction, and enumerate the many advantages that come from being able to trade these derivatives. The advantages include easy adjustment of market exposures, reduced transaction costs, same-day settlement or simultaneous trades, minimal disruption of underlying asset management strategies, and the ability to create specialized or custom risk–return patterns. The disadvantages of using derivatives include an increased monitoring burden as well as liquidity needed to meet margin requirements or for daily settlement of gains and losses.

Much of the monograph is devoted to explaining the various pricing formulae and payoff diagrams that characterize the derivatives markets. This technical material is extremely valuable to students and beginning practitioners who are unfamiliar with these markets.

The authors make special note of what has changed since the 1992 book. The biggest changes are the tremendous increase in the depth and liquidity of options and futures, an equally impressive increase in the number of underlying indices and assets, and the growth in international options and futures markets.

Scott D. Stewart, CFA, *Manager Selection*. Much of the literature on investing is concerned with selecting superior securities, in the spirit of Graham and Dodd, and with building portfolios of securities that maximize return for a given level of risk, in the spirit of Harry Markowitz. But most investors today operate one level removed from security selection: They choose *managers*.

As Scott D. Stewart, CFA, a professor at Boston University and former portfolio manager at Fidelity Investments, demonstrates in *Manager Selection*, building a portfolio of investment managers (institutional managers, mutual funds, or hedge funds) is like any other investment problem: It is a matter of identifying superior investments and building portfolios with them. At the fund level, however, a superior investment is not a company with attractive prospects or a cheap price; it is a fund managed by someone with skill. "Skill" has a peculiar meaning in this setting. It is not just knowledge or intelligence, which most fund managers have. It is also the ability to beat out other market participants in the quest for alpha (superior risk-adjusted return relative to an appropriately chosen benchmark), in a world where the sum of all manager alphas, before costs, is zero.

Stewart begins the book with advice on process and structure, a focus that anyone who has managed money will recognize as vitally important. Chapter 2 deals with the zero-sum nature of active management, as noted earlier, and discusses characteristics of successful, alpha-producing managers. The next chapter deals with index funds and the differences among index fund managers, including tracking error, costs, and qualitative factors.

Chapter 5, which draws on the mathematics in Grinold and Kahn's classic book *Active Portfolio Management*, discusses how to optimally combine active and index managers to form a portfolio. Chapter 6 covers performance measurement and related activities, and Chapter 7 reveals recent research findings, which I will discuss in greater detail below. In Chapter 8, Stewart provides assistance to the underserved community of financial advisers. The remainder of the book addresses alternative investments and draws general conclusions.

The research findings presented by Stewart in Chapter 7 include an evaluation of "soft" indicators of manager skill, such as tenacity, independent thinking, and hard work, as well as "hard" indicators, such as past performance and fees. He inquires whether alignment of incentives through performance fees is associated with higher returns; it is, very strongly, but the higher fees detract significantly from returns to the customer. In a later section of the chapter, Stewart discusses the track records of various categories of manager selectors. Retail (individual investor) fund selectors fare miserably; they tend to buy after a fund has earned good returns, but then they experience below-market returns. Institutional fund selectors, in contrast, do a little better; they earn, on average, zero (instead of negative) excess returns over the market after they buy.

Literature Reviews

Ronald J. Ryan, CFA, "The Evolution of Asset/Liability Management." Ronald J. Ryan, CFA, a fixed-income and multi-asset manager for pension funds, traces the evolution of asset/liability management (ALM) from cash flow dedication and immunization a generation ago through the current popularity of liability-driven investing. Frederick Macaulay, in 1938, laid the foundation for ALM by defining the duration of a bond and noting that duration measures a bond's interest rate sensitivity. A half-century later, Martin Leibowitz and his team of researchers at Salomon Brothers developed a more or less complete theory of ALM, detailed in a series of articles in the *Financial Analysts Journal* and other media.

More recently, as Ryan relates, defined benefit pension plans, which are supposed to be managed using ALM principles, have failed because the plans have become underfunded after years of poor stock market returns. ALM principles would have caused the plans to be invested primarily in fixed income, which rallied as the stock market fell. A new vocabulary of liability-driven investing (LDI) has arisen to implement both traditional ALM principles (buying fixed income and matching the duration of assets to that of liabilities) and multi-asset-class solutions. In the latter category is the modified capital asset pricing model (CAPM) of Waring and Whitney, who argue that a laddered portfolio of bonds or TIPS, rather than cash, is the true riskless asset when considered by an investor with a long-term liability. These authors, along with most others at the present time, suggest mixing risky assets with the riskless portfolio to enhance expected return.

Ryan concludes, however, by stating that, in the words of Fischer Black, "Almost every corporate pension fund should be entirely in fixed dollar investments."

Marianne M. Jennings, "Ethics and Financial Markets: The Role of the Analyst." Arizona State University Emeritus Law Professor Marianne Jennings addresses ethical issues faced by security analysts and others in a position to trade on inside information about stocks and other securities. Jennings distills ethical dilemmas down to three questions: "Does this violate the law? Is this honest? What if I were on the other side?" When analysts depart from asking these questions, she argues, ethical issues become entangled in a thicket of conflicting codes, laws, and regulations and it becomes difficult to arrive at a clear answer.

Jennings's perspective is historical and refers to codes of conduct as old as those of Hammurabi (c. 1750 BC) and the Old Testament. She describes the tulip bubble of the 1630s, the Buttonwood Agreement (which established brokers' oligopoly over securities trading in the United States), the panic of 1873, and Charles Ponzi's fraud in the 1920s.

The modern era of securities regulation begins in the 1930s in the aftermath of the crash of 1929–1932 and Great Depression. At about this time, a group of analysts in Chicago formed the first predecessor organization of CFA Institute. Jennings chronicles that organization's efforts to characterize security analysis as a profession instead of a business and to impose professional entrance requirements.

In more recent times, the emergence of a liquid junk bond market in the 1980s, a series of debt-related crises, the internet bubble of 1999–2002, and the real estate, mortgage, and stock market crash of 2008 contributed to public distrust of the markets. This crisis of confidence occurred at the same time that the public was becoming increasingly reliant on the markets as a savings and retirement security vehicle. Jennings details the "global settlement" that reined in the behavior of analysts and divorced their compensation from investment banking revenues.

Laurence B. Siegel
Gary P. Brinson Director of Research
The CFA Institute Research Foundation

Life Annuities: An Optimal Product for Retirement Income (a summary)

Moshe A. Milevsky
Published 2013 by the Research Foundation of CFA Institute
Summary prepared by Moshe A. Milevsky

To misquote the American comedian Rodney Dangerfield, annuities get very little respect. The public treats the word "annuity" with jaundice; the media often portray annuities as expensive and loaded with sales abuses; and the little respect they do receive tends to be from (a small group of) academic insurance economists, likely referring to an idealized mortality-contingent claim. Nonetheless, given aging and demographic trends, the decline in defined benefit pension coverage, and the widespread acknowledgment that current projections for government pension programs are in jeopardy, financial consultants, wealth managers, and asset allocators must prepare for their emerging role as *personal pension* managers. Accumulation and savings-oriented experts have to familiarize themselves with the unique financial challenges faced by retirees withdrawing money from their portfolios. In addition to addressing the standard behavioral and economic concerns, retirees and their advisers must now contend with longevity risk, sequence-of-returns risk, unique inflation risk, estate and income tax risk, and of course, medical expense risk. To get to the crux of the matter, I believe that life annuities are a core component of the optimal retirement income portfolio because they can effectively hedge many of these risks.

The purpose of this book is to familiarize nonexperts with the most important features, research, and literature on the topic of life annuities so that they can engage in meaningful and intelligent conversations with their clients. Chapter 1 provides a basic overview of the main institutional aspects of life annuities, Chapter 2 discusses more advanced and somewhat technical valuation issues, and Chapter 3 concludes the book with a comprehensive review of the scholarly financial and economic literature on life annuities.

At the most basic level, the life annuity can be viewed—and properly thought of—as a fixed-income bond that pays monthly coupons without a fixed maturity value or date. To the buyer, it looks like a portfolio of zero-coupon bonds structured to provide constant payments as long as the annuitant is still alive. The periodic payments may be level, increase at a predetermined rate, or be inflation indexed. Most importantly, the yield spread above the interest rate is generated by the mortality credits embedded in the risk pooling, a process that is explained within the book. The key message is that to replicate the enhanced life annuity yield by using conventional traded instruments (e.g., regular bonds) is virtually impossible. Moreover, for older people, the implied longevity yield is almost impossible to beat.

Of course, "annuity" is a catchall term that does not really mean anything until it is qualified with a proper label. Financial economists, securities lawyers, insurance executives, and members of the media often talk over each other and miss each other's points because they are referring to different products. For example, there are equity-indexed annuities, tax-deferred annuities, variable annuities (with and without guaranteed living benefits), fixed annuities, deferred annuities, and of course, fixed and variable immediate annuities. All of these products have the word "annuity" in their titles, but few offer the *raison d'être* of annuitization—that is, mortality credits. In fact, even the best low-cost variable and fixed immediate annuities (i.e., those that offer pure mortality credits) can be watered down if (1) guarantees, (2) period certain, or (3) refund options are added, which are unnecessary but often included to make the annuity product palatable to the loss-averse retiree.

Here is a useful way to think of the benefits of a life annuity: Imagine that you and a retired neighbor both invest $500 in a money market account, with the macabre proviso that the account can be cashed in only when one of you dies. The survivor gets the entire $1,000 plus any interest accrued, while the family of the deceased inherits nothing. (You may recognize this arrangement as a tontine.) Now, assuming you are the survivor, your terminal investment return on the $500—whatever and whenever that might be—will far exceed the investment return from conventional stocks or bonds during that period, even though the actual money was invested in cash. Of course, the key to the supercharged return from cash is that you have to survive to claim the mortality credits and assets of your neighbor. For the millions of Baby Boomers retiring on a meager pension and a depleted nest egg, however, this longevity-contingent claim or policy is likely to be the best hedge for their longevity risk. This policy is effectively asset/liability management on the personal balance sheet.

Another concept that is part of the life annuity dialogue is the notion of longevity risk tolerance or aversion. Longevity risk aversion is distinct from financial risk aversion; it is about the fear of living longer than expected and having to reduce your standard of living in retirement as a result. Individuals who are longevity risk averse will probably consume less of their wealth early in retirement and allocate more of their nest egg to annuity products to protect against this risk. This characteristic is akin to savers who are financially risk averse and who allocate more of their wealth to the safer assets, such as bonds. People who are financially risk averse are also likely to be longevity risk averse. In other words, counseling a retiree to buy more stocks because the person could live to be a centenarian might be internally inconsistent at best and an oxymoron at worst. Those who fear living a long time should own (more) life annuities.

Insurance economists would likely agree that life annuities, longevity insurance, and guaranteed pensions have an important role to play in the optimal retirement portfolio. Noted economists whose works are covered in the book have written extensively on the importance and role of these products in financing retirement, especially those retirees with minimal pension income from other sources. The debate in the literature tends to focus on (1) the optimal age of the annuitant, (2) the optimal amount invested, and (3) the optimal type of product. All of these researchers agree that life annuities are a legitimate and core product for the optimal retirement portfolio.

The fact that life annuities are priced in a competitive market to account for healthier, longer-lived individuals implies that an adverse selection cost is built into these insurance products. It is not a markup or loading, per se, but rather the reflection of a clientele interested in acquiring life annuities. Nevertheless, buying annuities as part of a group—or perhaps making annuities mandatory for a portion of your retirement account—would reduce the cost to everyone. If you can buy an insurance product in wholesale bulk as opposed to individual retail, you will save for two reasons. First, some fixed costs will be reduced; second, and more importantly, the adverse selection costs will be reduced.

Naturally, some individuals do not need any additional life annuities because they are already sufficiently annuitized or overannuitized. For example, anyone with a defined benefit pension plan from an employer already has a substantial portion of wealth preannuitized. If we add to this annuity social security benefits—which can add up to a $30,000 real, or inflation-adjusted, annuity per individual—many retirees do not need any more life annuity income. Moreover, if they have strong bequest motives, their optimal (additional) allocations to longevity-contingent claims should be close to zero. For high-net-worth individuals for whom social security provides only a tiny fraction of their cash flow needs in retirement but who are not so wealthy that they can really afford the legacy and bequest motives they assert, life annuities are an important class of products to consider.

Those who delay claiming U.S. Social Security (or Canada Pension Plan) income to the latest age possible are effectively buying a real (inflation-adjusted) advanced-life delayed annuity, with a survivor benefit for the spouse. The implied longevity yield from such a strategy far exceeds the rate of return available from real or nominal bonds in today's environment of ultra-low interest rates, especially for people in better-than-average health. For them, delaying annuitization is optimal.

Interestingly, behavioral evidence is growing that retirees (and seniors) who are receiving life annuity income are happier and more content with their financial condition in retirement than those receiving equivalent levels of income from other (fully liquid) sources, such as dividends, interest, and systematic withdrawal plans. Indeed, with growing concerns about dementia and Alzheimer's disease in an aging population, automatizing the retiree's income stream at the highest possible level—which is partly what a pension life annuity is all about—will become exceedingly important and valuable.

Credit risk, illiquidity, and low interest rates are three concerns that often are expressed by potential annuitants. Yet, all three concerns do not add up to an excuse for complete nonannuitization. The credit risk is mitigated by state guarantee funds. Annuitizing only a portion of your portfolio, for example, can solve the concern regarding liquidity and access to cash in the event of a medical emergency. In addition, fears about interest rates apply to any fixed-income instrument, not just life annuities.

In summary, as North American Baby Boomers march toward the random ends of their life cycles, the relatively small market of life annuities is likely to grow at much higher rates than it has in the past. This book endeavors to make this topic accessible to an audience that should (and perhaps must) know more about life annuities.

The complete book can be found at http://www.cfapubs.org/toc/rf/2013/2013/1.

Use your smartphone to scan the QR code to go straight to the webpage.

Fundamentals of Futures and Options (a summary)

Roger G. Clarke, Harindra de Silva, CFA, and
Steven Thorley, CFA
Published 2013 by the Research Foundation of CFA Institute
Summary prepared by Roger G. Clarke

Overview of Derivative Securities and Markets

The focus of this book is simple financial derivatives—options and futures. The growth of these instruments began in the United States, largely in the 1970s with the organization of the Chicago Board Options Exchange. Futures on U.S. Treasury bonds and notes began trading in the late 1970s, and options on individual stocks and equity indices began trading in the early 1980s. Since then, derivatives have not only expanded to other countries, but the set of underlying indices or assets has also grown. In many cases, the volume of trading in these instruments now exceeds the volume of trading in physical assets. In addition to derivatives of commodities and currencies, derivatives are now traded on a wide array of equity, interest rate, and credit indices; market volatility; inflation; weather; and real estate. Modeling the expected payoffs of many of these contracts requires complex calculations. Such calculations could not have been done without the increased data-handling capabilities and computing power available through modern computers. The growth in the development and use of the more complex derivatives has been an important trend in risk management and investing. In this book, however, we discuss only the relatively simple options and futures contracts. We leave the discussion of more complex derivatives to others.

Options and futures contracts are derivative instruments—that is, they derive their value from some other underlying security or index. The relationships between the underlying security and its associated options and futures contracts are illustrated in **Figure 1**. Note that options may be written on futures contracts but all options and futures ultimately derive their value from an underlying security or index. The links pictured in Figure 1 keep the security and its options and futures coupled together. The arbitrage link between a futures contract and the underlying security is called *spot–futures parity* or *cash-and-carry arbitrage*. The arbitrage linking put and call options to each other is referred to as *put–call parity*, which together with spot–futures parity links the options to the underlying security.

©2014 The CFA Institute Research Foundation

Figure 1. Arbitrage Links

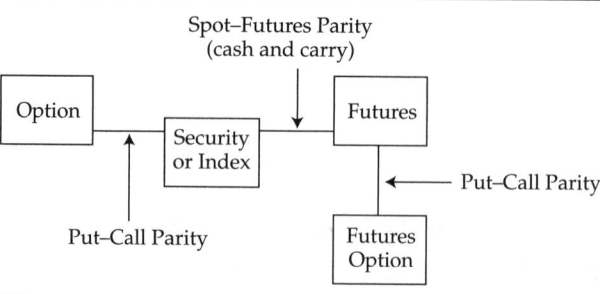

Standardized contract features allow futures and options to be traded quickly and efficiently on organized exchanges. The exchanges serve as intermediaries to facilitate trading, to transfer daily gains and losses between parties, and to pool resources of the exchange members to guarantee financial stability if a single investor should default. The individual parties to a given trade may never meet and do not need to deal with each other after an exchange has matched their trade. The exchange's clearinghouse function allows buyers or sellers to reverse a position before maturity and thus close out the obligation without having to find the party who initially took the other side of the trade.

The use of options and futures gives the investor flexibility in managing the risk of an underlying security or index. Such basic business activities as banking, international trading, and providing retirement benefits may leave an individual investor or corporation exposed to interest rate, foreign exchange, or equity market risk. The use of options and futures allows the investor to hedge or transfer all or some of this risk to others more willing to bear it. Derivative securities can also be used to speculate (assume risk) rather than hedge risk away, although most applications we discuss concern using them for risk control. The book focuses on contracts for financial assets, such as stocks, bonds, and foreign exchange, but structured derivative contracts exist for metals, energy, agricultural, and other physical commodities.

Trading in options and futures contracts has several potential operational advantages over trading in the underlying securities:

- easy adjustment of market exposure,
- reduced transaction costs,
- same-day settlement or simultaneous trades,
- less disruption of underlying asset management, and
- creation of specialized risk/return patterns.

Of course, the use of options and futures contracts also has some disadvantages:
- the need to understand complex relationships,
- potential tracking error to the underlying security or index,
- liquidity reserves required to post and meet margin requirements,
- daily settlement associated with marking to market, and
- potential short-term tax consequences.

Futures Contracts

A futures contract essentially allows an investor to commit now to the purchase or sale of an underlying asset at a specified price, with delivery and payment delayed until a specified settlement date. No money changes hands up front, except for posting initial margin to reduce the risk of nonpayment, but a futures contract can be either "bought" or "sold." The buyer of a futures contract has a *long position* and commits to buy the underlying asset or security at the specified price and date. The seller of a futures contract has a *short position* and commits to sell the underlying asset or security at the specified price and date. The fact that the future price for transacting is negotiated now but delivery and payment are delayed until the settlement date creates an *opportunity cost* for the seller in receiving payment. As a result, the negotiated price for future delivery of the asset differs from the current cash price by an amount that reflects the cost of waiting to get paid.

The futures price is related to the price of the underlying security or asset, the interest opportunity cost until expiration, and any expected cash distributions by the underlying asset before expiration. The futures price is tied to the price of the underlying security or index through the arbitrage condition of cash and carry. Because of arbitrage trading activity, when the underlying asset price changes, the price of the futures contract will change accordingly.

One way to think about the use of futures contracts is that the cash-and-carry arbitrage ensures that the futures contract plus a cash reserve will behave like the underlying security:

Futures + Cash ↔ Security.

Specifically, an investor may wish to create the same risk/return profile as the underlying security but use a futures contract because the transaction can be done more quickly and at less cost than buying or selling the underlying security. Such a process can be described as creating a *synthetic security* in place of the actual security.

In addition to creating a synthetic security, one can also rewrite the basic arbitrage relationship to create *synthetic cash*. In fact, creating a synthetic cash position is equivalent to hedging the underlying position in the security:

Security − Futures ↔ Cash.

The cash-and-carry arbitrage relationship keeps the futures contract priced so that an offsetting position relative to the underlying security results in a return to the hedger consistent with a riskless rate. In essence, creating a hedged position eliminates the primary risk in the underlying security by shifting it to others more willing to bear the risk. Of course, the investor's risk could be eliminated directly by simply selling the underlying security position, but this might interfere with the nature of the investor's business or disrupt a continuing investment program. Thus, the futures market provides an alternate way to temporarily offset or eliminate much of the risk in the underlying security position.

Option Contracts

The two basic types of options are *call* options and *put* options. A call option gives the owner the right to *buy* the underlying security at a specified price within a specified period of time. A put option gives the owner the right to *sell* the security at a specified price within a particular period of time. The *right*, rather than the obligation, to buy or sell the underlying security is what differentiates options from futures contracts.

In addition to buying an option, an investor may also sell a call or put option the investor had not previously purchased, which is often called *writing* an option. Thus, the two basic option positions can be expanded into four option positions, as shown in **Figure 2**. Understanding how put and call option prices behave and how these basic option positions affect an overall portfolio is critical to understanding more complex option strategies.

An exchange-traded option has a price at which it currently trades, sometimes called the option's *premium*. The option premium depends on a number of factors, including the difference between the option contract's *strike* or *exercise price* and the price of the underlying security. Analysts often describe

Figure 2. Option Positions

	Call Option	Put Option
Buy	Purchased the right to buy the underlying security	Purchased the right to sell the underlying security
Sell or Write	Sold the right to buy the underlying security (might be forced to sell)	Sold the right to sell the underlying security (might be forced to buy)

Fundamentals of Futures and Options (a summary)

the option's market price as being composed of two parts—the *intrinsic value* and the *time value*—as illustrated in **Figure 3**. In the case of a call option, the intrinsic value component, also called the *exercise value*, is the amount of money that would be received if an investor were to exercise the option to purchase the underlying security and then immediately sell the security at the current market price. In other words, the intrinsic value depends on the relationship between the current security price, S_0, and the exercise price of the option, X. If $S_0 - X$ is positive, then the call option is *in the money* and has a positive intrinsic value. If $S_0 - X$ is negative, then the call option is *out of the money* and has zero intrinsic value. Thus, the intrinsic value of a call option is the difference between the security price and the exercise price or zero, whichever is larger. The intrinsic value of a put option is just the reverse: the maximum of $X - S_0$ or zero, whichever is larger. For a put, the option is in the money if $X - S_0$ is positive; otherwise, the intrinsic value of the put option is zero.

The second component of the option price, the time value, is the difference or residual between the market price of the option and the current intrinsic value. As shown in Figure 3, the time value component of the option price is a function of the underlying security's expected volatility or risk, σ, the current level of interest rates, *r*, and the option's maturity date or time to expiration, *T*. The term *time value* comes from the fact that this component of the total option price gradually approaches zero as the option gets close to expiration, leaving only the intrinsic value. The convergence of the option price to the intrinsic value at expiration is similar to the convergence of a futures price to the underlying security price at expiration.

Figure 3. Option Price Components

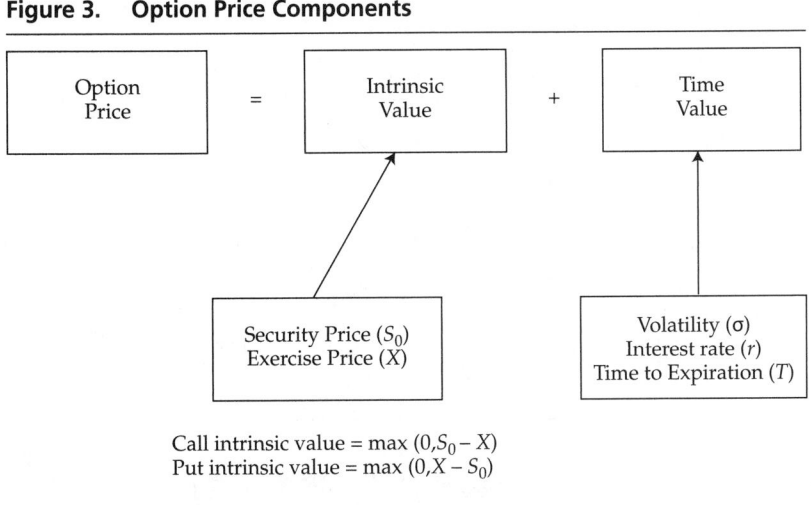

Call intrinsic value = max (0, $S_0 - X$)
Put intrinsic value = max (0, $X - S_0$)

©2014 The CFA Institute Research Foundation

Insight into the characteristics of options can be obtained by examining their payoff values at expiration. A *contingency table* is one technique for showing the expiration value of various option positions and strategies. The contingency table here shows the individual values of a long call, a long put, and the underlying security, contingent on whether the price of the security S_T is above or below the exercise price on option expiration date T.

	$S_T < X$	$S_T > X$
Call Option	0	$S_T - X$
Put Option	$X - S_T$	0
Security	S_T	S_T

As shown in this table, the call option has value at expiration if and only if the underlying asset price is above the strike price, X, and the put option has value at expiration if and only if the underlying asset price is below the strike price. The value of the underlying security, S_T, is not contingent on whether it is below or above the option's exercise price.

Another useful tool for option analysis is a *hockey stick* diagram of the option payoff at the expiration date as a function of the underlying asset price. For example, **Figure 4** illustrates the payoff pattern for a call option at expiration. The horizontal axis is the underlying security price, and the

Figure 4. Payoff Profile of a Call Option

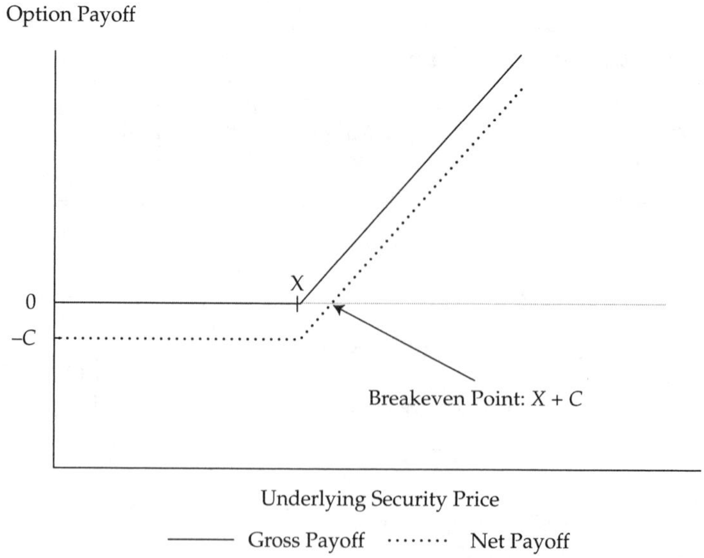

Fundamentals of Futures and Options (a summary)

vertical axis measures the gross payoff (solid line) and net payoff (dotted line) of the call option. If the security price ends up below the strike price, X, the gross payoff to the call option is zero, as shown on the left side of Figure 4. If the security price ends up above the exercise price, the gross payoff to the call option is the difference between the security price and the strike price, $S_T - X$, as shown on the right side of Figure 4. Because the investor must pay to initially purchase the option, the diagram includes a net payoff. The net payoff is the gross payoff of the option minus the initial purchase price, C_0.

The net payoff from the call option is a constant negative value until the security price reaches the exercise price. From that point, the net payoff starts to rise. The investor breaks even, with zero net profit, at the point where the security price equals the strike price plus the initial price paid for the option. Thus, the investor enjoys a positive net profit if the underlying asset price ends up being larger than the strike price plus the initial price paid for the option. Note that the call option payoff diagram has a kinked or asymmetrical payoff pattern, which distinguishes it from a futures contract. This asymmetry in the payoff allows the option to create specialized return patterns at expiration that are unavailable when using a futures contract.

Figure 5 is the payoff diagram for a put option. The put option has a gross payoff of zero if the underlying security price ends up above the exercise price, as shown on the right side of the diagram. If the underlying asset price is below

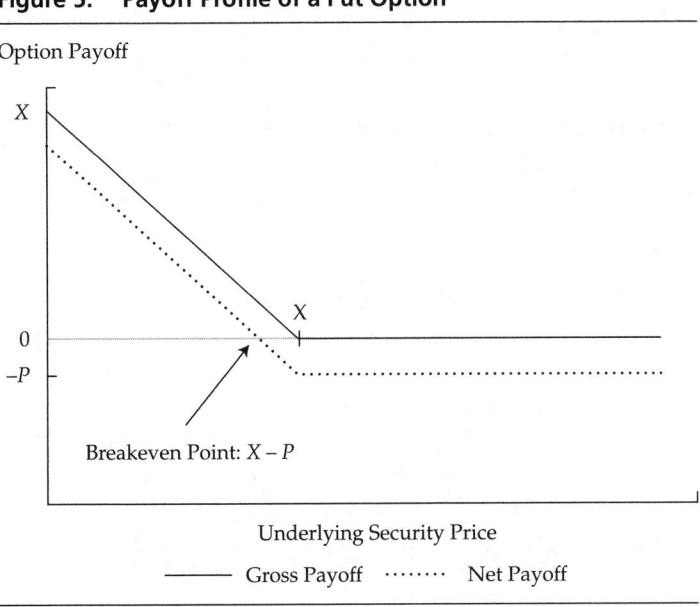

Figure 5. Payoff Profile of a Put Option

©2014 The CFA Institute Research Foundation 21

the strike price, the gross payoff to the put option is $X - S_T$, with the maximum gross payoff being X if the underlying security price goes all the way to zero. The net payoff is shown by the dotted line, which is shifted down from the gross payoff by the initial cost of the put option, P_0. The investor breaks even, with zero net profit, at the point where the security price equals the strike price minus the initial price of the put option. The investor in a put option incurs a net loss if the security price is above that value at the expiration of the option.

The payoff profiles for buying call and put options together with the payoff profiles for selling options can be used to better understand common option strategies. Commonly used strategies include covered calls, protective puts, and more involved option strategies, such as the straddle and the bull call spread.

Put–Call Parity

The arbitrage relationship for a call and put option pair for the same underlying security with the expiration dates is known as put–call parity. The basic form of the relationship can be written as the spread between the current price of a call option and the current price of the put option, which is equal to the spread between the current security price and a bond equal to the present value of the option strike price:

Call – Put = Security – Bond.

If the put–call parity relationship did not hold, one could create greater-than-riskless returns without any risk by selling the expensive combination of assets and buying the cheap combination. Thus, put–call parity is analogous to the cash-and-carry arbitrage condition for futures contracts, also known as spot–futures parity.

Algebraic perturbations of the basic put–call parity relationship can be used to provide insight into synthetic positions. For example, a common form of put–call parity that isolates the current price of the call option is

Call = Security + Put – Bond.

In this formulation, the call option can be thought of as being equal to the underlying security plus the corresponding put option minus a cash-equivalent security or riskless bond. In other words, a *synthetic* call option can be created by buying the security and the put option, where most (although not all) of the cost is covered by borrowing the present value of X dollars. Specifically, the combination of securities on the right side of the equation would produce the same payoff as buying the call option directly.

Another perturbation of the put–call parity relationship,

Put = Call + Bond – Security,

shows that an investor can create a synthetic put option by buying the call option and investing the present value of *X* dollars at the risk-free rate, where most (although not all) of the cost is covered by the proceeds from shorting the underlying security. Again, the combination of securities on the right side would produce the same payoff as buying the put option directly.

In fact, the payoff of the underlying security itself can be replicated by buying a riskless bond with a face value of *X*, buying a call option, and writing a put option. In a similar way, a riskless bond can be constructed by buying the underlying security, buying a put option, and selling a call option.

We can also leave *two* terms on each side of the put–call parity formula to create a synthetic covered-call position:

Security − Call = Bond − Put.

On the left side of the equation, the traditional covered-call position is established by buying the security and selling the call option, but the right side indicates that an equivalent position is to buy a riskless bond at a discount with a face value of *X* and sell the put option.

Finally, a synthetic protective put can be created by buying a riskless bond at a discount with face value *X* and buying a call option:

Security + Put = Bond + Call.

Option Pricing

Option prices depend on the price of the underlying security, the strike price of the option, the volatility of the underlying security, the level of interest rates, and the option's time to expiration. Fully understanding the impact of each of these parameters requires a model of the option price, not simply a decomposition of the price into the intrinsic value and time value components. The book reviews the pricing of options through the use of a binomial branching process that allows the investor to price put and call options on the basis of their parameters and the assumed distribution of returns to the underlying security. In the limit, as the branching process is expanded, the binomial pricing logic converges to various forms of the well-known Black–Scholes model.

Specifically, the formula for a European-style call option (an option that can be exercised only on the maturity date) on an underlying asset without cash distributions prior to option expiration is

$$C_0 = S_0 N(d_1) - Xe^{-rT} N(d_2),$$

where

$$d_1 = \frac{\ln(S_0/X) + (r + \sigma^2/2)T}{\sigma\sqrt{T}}$$

and

$$d_2 = \frac{\ln(S_0/X) + (r - \sigma^2/2)T}{\sigma\sqrt{T}}.$$

The Black–Scholes formula uses a number of functions associated with *continuous time* financial mathematics. For example, the function $N(\ )$ is the cumulative standard normal distribution and the function $\ln(\ )$ is the natural logarithm, with $e^{(\ )}$ as the corresponding exponentiation function. In continuous-time mathematics, present values are calculated by the term e^{-rT} instead of the more familiar $1/(1+R)^T$ formulation used in discrete-time mathematics.

Option analysts use a series of Greek letters to describe how a call option price changes as the various parameters change. The most important "greek" is *delta*, Δ, which describes the change in the option price as a result of a change in the price of the underlying security. The delta of an option is also known as the *hedge ratio* because it specifies the number of shares in the underlying security needed to offset a change in option value resulting from changes in the underlying security price. Another greek is *theta*, θ, the change in option price arising from the passage of time. Other greeks that are used are also discussed in the book.

The existence of option contracts across a range of strike prices for a single underlying security allows option analysts to measure aspects of the probability distribution for the underlying security's return that are not directly observable without options markets. Similarly, option contracts with different expiration dates can be used to forecast how the volatility of the underlying security is expected to evolve over time. These advanced probability-distribution and term-structure-of-volatility perspectives both use the concept of *implied volatility*, which is defined as the volatility parameter that justifies a quoted option price. The volatilities implied from options on market indices are now routinely provided, in addition to the levels of the indices themselves, as market indicators. For example, VIX is the volatility implied by the price for options on the S&P 500 Index.

In summary, the use of options contracts can be an important tool for managing investment risk.

* * * * * *

The complete monograph can be found at http://www.cfapubs.org/toc/rf/2013/2013/3.

Use your smartphone to scan the QR code to go straight to the webpage.

Manager Selection (a summary)

Scott D. Stewart, CFA
Published 2013 by the Research Foundation of CFA Institute
Summary prepared by Scott D. Stewart, CFA

The Importance of Manager Selection

Manager selection is a critical step in implementing any investment program. Even though investment objectives may be finalized and targets for asset class weights set, an investment plan is not productive until it is implemented through the purchase or sale of securities, properties, commodities, and derivatives. In most cases, investors choose portfolio managers to determine the most appropriate instruments in which to place assets. Investors hire portfolio managers to act as their agents, and portfolio managers are trusted to perform to the best of their abilities and in the investors' best interests.

Investors must practice due diligence when selecting index managers or active portfolio managers. Investors want managers who are highly skilled, diligent, and persistent, and they also want managers whose interests are aligned with their own. But investors need to do more than identify skillful managers; they need to determine the appropriate weights to assign to those managers.

The goal of this book is to help investors improve their practice of manager selection. It highlights the influence that investment policy statements have on manager selection and proposes techniques for hiring active, indexed, and alternative managers. Strategies for setting portfolio manager weights are also reviewed, along with techniques for monitoring current managers. A large part of the book is devoted to providing an in-depth look at the value of quantitative and qualitative methods for successful manager selection. Special issues for financial advisers and individual investors are also addressed. The book concludes with a summary of key recommendations.

How Manager Selection Fits within the Investment Process

An investment policy statement (IPS) has important implications for manager selection. It should include a description of the client or investor, the overall mission, and the goals for investing. It should also document the investment objectives that the investor considers most relevant in determining appropriate managers and setting relationship expectations.

Investors' views, horizons, sizes, and experiences influence the formulation of an IPS and, in turn, affect the selection process. For example, investors' liquidity needs, quality preferences, and risk guidelines will constrain the search for appropriate managers. Investors should carefully consider the implications for manager selection when formulating their IPS.

Identifying Skilled Active Managers

If we gather the returns of all portfolios—both indexed and active, institutional and retail—and weight them by their values, the result (before fees and transaction costs) will equal the return on the market. If all portfolios are not identical in composition, some will exhibit performance that is higher than the market and some will exhibit lower performance. Empirical evidence supports these conclusions, but the estimates must be prepared with care. For example, many portfolios are not publicly observable.

The arithmetic of active management illustrates that some managers will outperform or underperform market averages. The efficient market hypothesis questions whether any manager has the ability to create alpha. Given a large sample of managers, it should not be difficult to find some with performance records that appear to reflect statistically significant alphas. But this approach ignores the fact that the best performing managers are cherry-picked from the market sample. Based on sophisticated tests, it appears that skillful managers do exist, but the number of managers that demonstrate skill with high statistical confidence appears to be small.

This book details the techniques investors use for selecting active managers and reports on their effectiveness. For example, there is evidence that alphas persist at least for a short time. There is also evidence that superior scores on aptitude tests are positively correlated with superior investment performance. But there is no guaranteed method to identify managers who will outperform in the future. In fact, evidence shows that both retail and institutional investors on average do not profit from their manager hiring and firing processes.

Index Fund Investing

The goal of investing in index funds is to replicate the performance of a pre-specified equity or fixed-income benchmark. Index managers provide investors with inexpensive access to returns on the market. The term "passive management" is sometimes used to describe indexing, but it does not reflect the skill that index fund managers need to have to deliver accurate results, which in many cases are defined by deviations of a few basis points relative to published indices. This book reports that index fund performance, net of fees, shows evidence of persistence; therefore, investors can improve their selection process by reviewing managers' historical record of benchmark tracking.

Asset Allocation Policy and Its Implications for Manager Selection

The asset allocation process entails setting optimal weights of broad classes of securities, such as stocks and bonds, within a portfolio. The more complex a set of assets is, the more effort will be required for manager selection. For example, selecting a large-cap equity index fund is a relatively straightforward process, whereas private equity investing requires a thorough and lengthy process of due diligence of managers and partnerships. This book recommends that investors consider the implications for the manager selection process when formulating their strategic asset allocation policies.

Setting Weights for Active and Index Managers

The manager selection process involves conducting due diligence, identifying the most skillful managers, and determining the proportion of assets each manager should control. Investors set manager weights to meet strategic asset allocation goals, capture alpha potential of active managers, and access the tracking abilities of index managers.

Determining optimal mixes of portfolio managers is dependent on investors' expectations for alphas, their attitudes toward active risk, and managers' risk exposures. Investors may seek optimal trade-offs between active return and active risk or, alternatively, maximize active return while holding active risk to an acceptable level. This optimization problem can be expressed as a mathematical model and is illustrated in the book by using a case study and a Microsoft Excel template that investors can use to set manager weights.

The Dynamics of Manager Selection: Performance Analysis, Monitoring, and Fee Incentives

Investors' horizons, market characteristics, and manager alphas all vary over time. Ideally, an IPS should specify prompts, independent of performance, for conducting special reviews of current managers. Investment professionals should avoid hiring managers at the top of their performance cycle and should use several different tools to evaluate their managers over time. These include tools to estimate alphas, compute performance attribution, and evaluate fee structures, including performance-based schedules. These issues are reviewed, and an Excel template is included to explain how to estimate manager alphas.

Research Findings on Manager Selection

Finance research literature explores whether active managers earn statistically significant alphas, whether alphas persist once found, and whether investors profit from hiring and terminating investment managers. This book contains a chapter that summarizes research on portfolio managers and entrepreneurs (who share traits with portfolio managers) and outlines manager selection techniques that have been shown to be successful in the past.

Issues for Financial Advisers

Individual investors, including high-net-worth and retirement investors, face more challenges than institutional investors in successful manager selection. They are subject to higher expenses, including taxes, and have less time to focus on investing. Individual investors are often less sophisticated and less experienced than institutional investors and, as a result, often seek the support of financial advisers. Several approaches are proposed for financial advisers to improve their manager selection processes.

Manager Selection for Global Markets and Alternative Asset Classes

The manager selection process is more complex for global investing than for domestic investing, and the same holds true for alternative versus traditional investing. This book reviews research evidence on active global equity, private equity, and hedge fund investments and proposes techniques for selecting managers for these asset classes.

Key Recommendations and Best Practices

The final chapter of the book summarizes key recommendations for manager selection, including advice shared by experienced investors, pension consultants, and money managers.

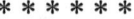

The complete monograph can be found at http://www.cfapubs.org/toc/rf/2013/2013/4.

Use your smartphone to scan the QR code to go straight to the webpage.

Ethics and Financial Markets: The Role of the Analyst (a summary)

Marianne M. Jennings
Published 2013 by the Research Foundation of CFA Institute
Summary prepared by Marianne M. Jennings

The ethical issues financial analysts face today are no different from the ethical issues financial advisers, fund managers, and analysts have faced over the decades and centuries that financial markets have existed. A review of the history of ethics in investment markets, as well as the literature related to that history and the profession, points to two conclusions: (1) History does repeat itself, and (2) when analysts depart from three simple questions (Does this violate the law? Is this honest? What if I were on the other side?), complex issues are resolved through a thicket of codes, laws, and regulations that encourage further interpretations and exceptions and cloud judgment.

This historical perspective is designed to bring about the introspection that prevents repetition of the same ethical missteps and permits progress through ethical practices and the resulting enhancement of professional reputation.

The Long Journey from Hammurabi to 1929

Ethics in the marketplace is not a new concept. In fact, fraud has been and always will be with us. The Code of Hammurabi covered everything from adultery to business trade, with the basic goal of the code being to impose harm on the perpetrator equal to the harm done to the customer/client. Imagine the same principle applied to investment advisers whose clients experienced collapsed investment portfolios: If you lose their money, you lose yours too.

It is clear from the Bible that fraud was afoot because we find this warning in Leviticus 25:14: "And if thou sell ought unto thy neighbor, or buyest ought of thy neighbor's hand, ye shall not oppress one another" (from the King James Version of the Bible). The modern translation would be that selling short is wrong if you have inside information that earnings for the company's stock are going to go down.

In the roughly 1,400 years between that warning and the time of the prophet Ezekiel, there was apparently not much improvement. Ezekiel warned: "The people of the land have used oppression, and exercised robbery, and have vexed the poor and needy: Yea, they have oppressed the stranger wrongfully"

(King James Version of the Bible, Ezekiel 22:29). Oppression is translated as fraud, and apparently, it was a problem during the eras when we did not even have running water. Strangers were taken advantage of by those trying to sell, sell, sell. Market sophistication changes, but the problem of taking advantage of others is too often still at the root of all collapsed investments.

About 2,000 years after Ezekiel, investors faced the great tulip market bubble of 1636, which is the earliest documented bubble in a market. When the tulip was developed, people were enamored by it. They began buying tulips, fields of tulips, and developing tulips. When tulips were no longer available, they began buying tulip bulbs because they would have a tulip at some time in the future. When there were no bulbs left, they created a market for tulip bulb futures.

Eventually, investors realized that those who sold the futures could not possibly deliver bulbs for all those futures that had been sold, and the market collapsed. The story of the world's first market bubble is eerily similar to each bubble since then. At the time, investors could have purchased 24 tons of wheat (tangible goods) for the cost of one tulip bulb future. The event thus illustrates how the drive to succeed in a bull market clouds judgment and compromises honesty.

The institution we call "Wall Street" was born in 1792 through the Buttonwood Agreement by an association of brokers, which eventually developed into the New York Stock & Exchange Board and then into the New York Stock Exchange (NYSE). The first scandal to take banks down was the Duer and Malcomb land scandal, resulting in public outrage and cries for morality in the marketplace.

1863–1913: The New York Stock Exchange Grows and Then Panics—Hearings Result. The 1863–1913 time period was an era that witnessed expansive investment in the country's infrastructure (railroads), followed by the Panic of 1873. The panic resulted from investors' realization that the speculative investments in railroads, this era's equivalent of the tulip bulb, were worthless. Investors had been taken in by the railroad expansion, and overbuilding resulted; think real estate speculation. Advisers, however, continued to tout railroad investments long after it was clear that tracks and facilities had been overbuilt. The result was the sale of junk-quality bonds.

When the railroad bubble burst, more than 100 railroads declared bankruptcy. Public outrage over the event resulted in a change in political parties in the subsequent federal elections. A lasting result was a "general distrust" of Wall Street among investors as well as bank customers.

The states subsequently attempted regulation because of the perception that the federal government lacked the authority to regulate financial markets. The first significant state securities law was passed in Kansas in 1911. It was an antifraud statute that resulted in similar laws in other states, referred to as "blue sky laws" because they were designed to prevent swindlers who were so bold that they "would sell building lots in the blue sky."

1920s: From Ponzi Schemes to Investment Trusts. Charles Ponzi left both his mark and his name in the financial markets with his use of arbitrage via the pricing disparity in stamps between Spain and the United States. But the 1920s was still a period of tremendous market growth fueled by shares in investment trusts—a form of auction-rate securities, the same types of securities that investment banks would sell to clients nearly 100 years later.

By 1927, the NYSE saw what the Kansas legislature had already seen: The information investors had was neither forthright nor forthcoming. The NYSE responded to the need for better disclosure in stock offerings by imposing filing requirements on its members before they would be permitted to list securities for sale on the exchange.

Nonetheless, the leveraged market structure became more leveraged with each additional offering of investment trusts. The initial purchases had to continue to show investors that the demand for these trust securities continued. When the stock market crashed in 1929, investors who had bought into the "safe" investment trusts were left with worthless investments. Those who had lent money to the investment banks were left with worthless collateral and debtors lacking not only cash but also assets. The Dow dropped 89% by 1932.

Securities Regulation: 1933 and 1934 Legislation

The post-1929 congressional hearings on the market crash examined the activities of investment firms as well as the analysts who had touted the investment trust instruments as being safe. The Pecora hearings of 1932 represented a turning point in market regulations and was a time when the public was riveted by the disclosures and testimony before the Senate Banking Committee. Ferdinand Pecora was chief counsel to the United States Senate Committee on Banking and Currency during its investigation after the market crash.

By the time of the Pecora hearings, the market was nearing its bottom, 89%. Pecora's focus on the ethical and moral character of the businesses and professionals on Wall Street resulted in the market's most substantial reforms in its history.

The results of the conduct of the investment industry during the bull market, the resulting 1929 crash, and the revelations in congressional hearings about the conduct of banks, investment professionals, and company executives were the Banking Act of 1933 (the Glass–Steagall Act) and the Securities Act of 1933 (for the regulation of primary offerings), which was then followed by the Securities Exchange Act of 1934 (for regulation of the secondary markets) and the creation of the Securities and Exchange Commission.

1934–1959: Investment Market Reforms—Voluntary Action and Professional Ethics

The 1934–59 era was one of introspection for some members of the profession because of the impact the hearings had on the public's perception of analysts and their trust in markets. In addition, there was unprecedented volatility in the markets following the 1929 crash. It was as if perceptive analysts took the lessons of the Pecora hearings and embraced an Edgar Allan Poe resolve of "never more."

In 1925, a group of Chicago investment analysts began meeting for lunch to discuss the issues facing their profession. Slowly, national professional groups developed, along with ethical standards and the perceived need for entrance requirements, a code of ethics, and disciplinary procedures for members. By 1947, the city-based groups had decided to form a multinational organization (the United States and Canada were first to be included) to advance their mission of improving standards and ethics within the industry. The national group that resulted was the Financial Analysts Federation (FAF).

1959–1974: Professional Entrance Requirements and Soft Dollars Begin

In 1959 the FAF created the Institute of Chartered Financial Analysts (ICFA) and charged it with developing and keeping current a body of knowledge that would help members understand the issues in the industry. The ICFA was also given the responsibility of developing a rigorous examination (roughly 10% of which focused on ethical issues) that would be required for members to use the CFA designation following their names.

As the FAF was proceeding with its efforts to increase both ethics and professionalism in investment markets, the structure of the market itself was creating different types of ethical issues. One particular issue emerged that remains with the investment industry today—soft dollars. The practice of paying "soft dollars" began in the 1950s, when the investment brokers and traders operated under fixed, nonnegotiable commission rates, which were probably too high.

Even as this seemingly free offer of research took hold, an ethical issue gnawed at fund managers: Were they compromising their fiduciary duties to their beneficiaries by accepting the free research?

1975: May Day and Soft Dollars Expand

In 1975, Congress amended the 1934 Securities Exchange Act to deregulate commission rates on Wall Street. May Day 1975 (as this move was called because of the date of the change) meant that the NYSE price controls were eliminated to ease the soft dollar tension. The unintended consequence of the deregulation, however, was that ethical issues became more acute because pricing differentials still included the formerly unpriced research services. The soft dollar concept was now institutionalized because the commissions and research services were bundled together. Changes in federal law did, however, address the ethical concerns for fund managers with regard to the issue of fiduciary duty should they opt to pay a higher commission rate because of the research benefits.

1980–1990: Public Distrust from Analyst Practices

The 1980s was a decade of headline ethical lapses, including the Dirks and Boesky insider-trading cases as well as the Milken junk bond issues. These cases captured the public's attention because fictional Gordon Gekko's mantra of "greed is good" fueled backlash about investment markets.[1] The perception of an unfair playing field or asymmetrical dissemination of information to movers and shakers or by analysts to lucky clients perpetuated a public unease about the profession.

1991–2002: The Dot-Com Bubble and Collapse, and the Global Settlement

Throughout the 1990s, soft dollar arrangements went largely undisclosed and/or misunderstood by fund beneficiaries, even as academics, the media, and regulators were raising questions about the lack of transparency, their real cost, and the independence of the research being furnished through the arrangements.

In 1992, the *Wall Street Journal*, reporting on the realities of investment banking operations, indicated that the so-called Chinese wall (said to separate the analyst/research side of the brokerage house and the investment banking and trading side of the house) was imaginary. Some analysts were told to avoid negative statements about clients of the firm. In addition, analysts were expected to do more than simply offer favorable ratings. Analysts were told to "pound the table" to sell the stocks that they had rated favorably. As the popular business press continued its investigative reporting on actual analyst practices, academic studies began to appear with the same conclusion: There was an inherent bias between investment bankers and analysts.

As the many-faceted debate over soft dollars and independence continued, the market was building a bubble. The confidence of a bull market in evolving technology resulted in initial public offerings (IPOs) and stock offerings by companies that had not yet shown any earnings but that had been blessed with favorable ratings from analysts housed at the investment banking firms that were

---

[1]The quote from the movie *Wall Street* (1987) was actually taken from a May 1986 commencement address Ivan Boesky gave at Berkeley in which he said, "Greed is all right.... Greed is healthy. You can be greedy and still feel good about yourself." As quoted in Christopher R. Brauchli, "From the Wool-Sack," *Colorado Lawyer* (August 2002):43.

leading the IPOs. Then-chairman of the SEC Arthur Levitt publicly expressed concern about the role of analysts in touting stocks their firms were offering.

When the bubble burst, in tandem with the Enron, Tyco, and other ethical collapses, the SEC promulgated Regulation Fair Disclosure (hereafter, Regulation FD). The regulation was designed to curb the practice of disclosing pertinent information to a select set of analysts and investors. Believed to be a tool for firms to influence institutional investors and curry favor with superstar analysts, selective disclosure had long been criticized as a scourge plaguing information dissemination.

The end result of the dot-com bubble was what is known as the "global settlement," which resulted in the following changes in the profession:

- Analyst compensation cannot be tied to specific investment banking transactions.
- Analysts' personal trading is restricted in securities of companies they are following for their firms.
- Analysts cannot offer favorable research in exchange for business for their firms.
- Investment banking review of analysts' research reports is restricted.
- Quiet periods have been designated for the issuance of research reports.

2002–2007: The Real Estate/Mortgage Bubble

The same critical question that arose following the end of market runs in the other eras arose in 2002–2007: How was so much that was so obvious neither discussed nor disclosed for so long? The simple answer to the question is that many were aware, particularly those who were analysts, but they suppressed their concerns rather than disclosing them publicly. In fact, the documentation of concerns among analysts and others involved in the sales and evaluation of these securities during this era was greater than the documentation found from previous financial collapses, including even the modern Enron and dot-com eras.

2008–2012: The Financial Crisis and Reforms, Expert Networks, Pension Crises, Municipal Bankruptcies, and Insider Trading

The 2008–12 period was an era of regulatory reform. The Dodd–Frank Wall Street Reform and Consumer Protection Act was passed in 2010 and created the Financial Stability Oversight Council (FSOC) to monitor the financial health of financial institutions. Dodd–Frank brought to analysts the same types of changes that Sarbanes–Oxley had imposed on accountants and auditors in 2007.

As those reforms proceeded, new issues involving analysts emerged. This period was full of news articles on insider-trading arrests and resulting "perp walks" because of the so-called expert networks and their interconnections with research firms and hedge funds.

The Common Ethical Threads of the Ethical Eras

This review of investment market eras shows us that history repeats and that the ethical issues that affect investment markets have not changed and are not yet resolved with clear standards. The issues of soft dollars, insider trading, conflicts of interest, and unprofessional conduct remain with us.

* * * * * *

The complete literature review, which contains 94 annotated citations on the relevant research, can be found at http://www.cfapubs.org/toc/rflr/2013/8/1.

Use your smartphone to scan the QR code to go straight to the webpage.

The Evolution of Asset/Liability Management (a summary)

Ronald J. Ryan, CFA
Published 2013 by the Research Foundation of CFA Institute
Summary prepared by Ronald J. Ryan, CFA

The objective of most US institutions with assets to invest is to fund some sort of liability, as is the case with banks, insurance companies, pension funds, and so forth. As a result, asset/liability management (ALM) should be the investment focus and the basis for selecting the core portfolio.

Insurance companies may be the birthplace of ALM and certainly have been the model of ALM discipline, thanks to the heavy regulations imposed on them. IAIS Standard No. 13 (International Association of Insurance Supervisors 2006) defines asset/liability management as the practice of managing a business so that decisions and actions taken with respect to assets and liabilities are coordinated. Therein lies the essence of proper ALM: It should be an orchestrated event based on enhancing the funded ratio (assets/liabilities). It should not have any other objective or interference, such as generic market indices, peer group comparisons, or inflation. In short, ALM can be defined as the process that deals with interest rate risk management.

Banks and insurance companies have practiced ALM since their inception. Their ALM approach centers on the interest rate risk management of assets versus liabilities such that their risk/reward behavior is similar or matched. Financial theory offers no good reason for making a distinction between ALM as practiced by banks, insurance companies, or pensions. So, the time has come to stop treating pensions as anything different or special. In this sense, all liabilities are similar or have the same systematic risk—namely, interest rate risk. Therefore, ALM as practiced by banks and insurance companies should apply to pensions as well.

The focus of this literature review is the evolution of ALM for pensions. One noticeable feature of pensions is that they have no regulations requiring asset/liability management or the matching of assets to liabilities. This lack of regulation may be the most important cause of the ballooning pension deficits of the past 13 years.

In the Beginning: Dedication

The history of formal ALM for pensions (sometimes referred to as liability-driven investing, or LDI) is littered with false starts. Dedication was the earliest form of ALM for pensions. It was in vogue during the historically high interest rate environment of the late 1970s and early 1980s. And because it required the exact matching of a stream of cash inflows (assets) to a stream of cash outflows (liabilities), dedication was referred to as "cash matching."

The dedication model required a sophisticated computer program to perform the many iterations necessary to achieve efficient cash flow matching by leaving the least amount of cash flow uninvested or unmatched. The model assumed a 100% bond portfolio held to maturity or to the liability payment dates (termination dates). The quest was thus to find the least expensive collection of bonds to perform this future-value matching.

Dedication had several distinct advantages:

1. Certain or predictable cash flows (when held to maturity).
2. Risk reduction (market, reinvestment, inflation, default, and liquidity).
3. Specificity (asset cash flows must match liability cash flows).
4. Simple asset allocation (100% bonds).
5. Passive asset management (more certain returns with lower fees).

Dedication also had several disadvantages, which, in time, may have led to its failure as the core strategy for pension plans:

1. The model is not easy to construct. At the time, sophisticated computer models were expensive and intellectually challenging. These models thus became the domain of broker/dealers, who eliminated many asset managers or competitors.
2. The complicated mathematical models are hard for many pension plan sponsors to understand.
3. The model is dependent on accurate projected liability benefit payments (cash outflows). This problem introduced a strain, or risk factor, for actuaries and uncertainty with regard to model inputs.
4. The model is designed to match future values, not present values. This issue creates potential volatility for funded ratios (which are based on present values or market values) if asset market values do not behave in sync with liability market values.
5. The model reduces—or even eliminates—the role of active bond managers for asset management and the role of pension consultants for asset allocation.
6. The transaction cost of dedication was highly interest rate sensitive (inversely correlated), so as the secular trend to lower rates continued from 1982 onward, dedication became increasingly more expensive to execute.

Immunization Replaces Dedication as an ALM Strategy

Future-value matching of liabilities (dedication) is most beneficial for accounting purposes when there is a certain, or guaranteed, match of assets to liabilities. To execute a certain match of liabilities requires zero-coupon bonds matched to the liability payment dates and amounts. But because zero-coupon bonds were not available until 1985 (with the introduction of Treasury STRIPS), it was mathematically difficult for dedication models using coupon bonds to be a certain, or guaranteed, match of liabilities because of reinvestment risk, call risk, or anything that would alter the cash flows.

Dedication thus gave way to immunization, which was designed to consistently match the present value growth behavior of liabilities because that is how the accounting rules (Statement of Financial Accounting Standards Nos. 87 and 158) measure the funded ratio of a plan. This approach also reduced the volatility of contribution costs, which are based on the funded ratio.

Immunization focused on matching the interest rate sensitivity of liabilities in present value dollars. As a result, it focused on duration (or modified duration) in harmony with horizon analysis. Duration measures the average life of a security (asset or liability) in present value dollars. When it is modified (Negative of duration/1 + Yield to maturity), duration is a fair proxy for price return movement given an interest rate movement. Although duration is an old concept (from 1938), it never got much attention until ALM under immunization came in vogue in the late 1970s and early 1980s, when academic papers on immunization, duration, and dedication began to appear in increasing numbers.

As interest rates rose in a long secular trend from 1974 to 1982, the financial industry began to pay more and more attention to duration. Realizing that the high interest rates would allow them to lock in unprecedented rates of return, defined benefit pension fund managers embraced the concepts of dedication and then immunization. Wall Street broker/dealers—especially Salomon Brothers, with Martin Leibowitz as its intellectual leader—provided the complicated software models to execute dedication and immunization effectively. Many papers promoting and critiquing immunization strategies were written by quantitative scholars during this time.

Things were good for the broker/dealers who could execute very large dedication and immunization portfolios. Perhaps the largest bond trades ever recorded were those done for dedication and immunization as single, very large orders. Things were not so good, however, for the many active bond managers and pension consultants who saw their clients' need for active bond managers and asset allocation models dwindling.

As interest rates began to fall in early 1982, call risk began to surface as a serious impediment to immunization and dedication models, especially for those who ventured into mortgage-backed securities. This prepayment and call risk altered cash flows and maturity structures, which damaged the integrity of immunization and dedication models dependent on these certain cash flows and maturity dates.

As a solution to the problems with immunization, Salomon Brothers offered a new financial theory it called "contingent immunization." Salomon declared contingent immunization to be a form of active management. (It was actually a blend of active and passive management.) The procedure allowed for the pursuit of active bond management within a framework that provided a minimum return, even under adverse experience.

This minimum return was achieved through a procedural safety net based on the techniques of bond immunization. The portfolio stayed in active management mode as long as the portfolio's asset value placed it above this safety net, and it entered the immunization or passive management mode only when absolutely necessary to ensure a promised minimum return. Contingent immunization seemed to offer the best of both worlds—the pursuit of maximum returns through active management and the limitation of downside risk through immunization.

Accounting Rules Redirect Pension Asset Management

When the Financial Accounting Standards Board (FASB) issued its Statement of Financial Accounting Standards No. 87 (FAS 87) in 1985, effective December 1986, it created both a good and a bad moment in the evolution of asset/liability management. It clarified that the discount rate methodology used for liabilities should be based on a high-quality bond yield curve that settles the liabilities. Because immunization strategies focused on matching the present values, a major consideration became what discount rates to use to calculate the present value of liabilities. FAS 87 helped those using immunization strategies understand how to price and match the present value of liabilities. Notably, FAS 87 allowed corporations to use the return on asset (ROA) assumption to offset pension expense. As a result, if the dollar growth in pension assets based on the ROA rate exceeded the pension expense amount, then pension expense would become pension income (or credit), which would directly enhance earnings. Because corporations are earnings per share (EPS) driven and not liability driven, the ROA—instead of matching and funding liabilities—soon became the hurdle rate or objective return of pension assets.

When interest rates went below the ROA assumption rate (roughly 8%) in the late 1980s, dedication and immunization strategies fell out of vogue because they supposedly would have locked in a return that was not sufficient to neutralize or overcome pension expense, thereby causing an EPS drain. As a result, dedication and immunization were largely replaced by surplus optimization strategies, which aimed for the growth of pension assets to outpace liability growth, thus creating a pension surplus that would reduce or even eliminate contribution costs.

Contribution requirements are a function of the funded ratio (the ratio of plan assets to liabilities, in present value terms). The size or present value of the liability is sensitive to the discount rate used to reduce future benefit payments to a present value. (Specific methods for determining the discount rate are discussed later.) The sponsor is thus required to make contributions such that the plan will be fully funded over a time horizon specified by law.[1]

The late 1980s and the decade of the 1990s were good times for pensions. By switching to a surplus optimization strategy, asset allocation models favored equities over bonds because the ROA was now the bogey or growth benchmark. This asset allocation decision worked out well during this period: Equities enjoyed several good years of double-digit returns, resulting in pension surpluses, which enhanced EPS (returns above the ROA were an "actuarial gain" line item that increased EPS) and reduced or eliminated contribution costs. ALM thus became a hard sell given the level of interest rates, the historical return track record of equities, and the resulting financial statement benefits of an ROA hurdle rate. But this focus on absolute return (ROA) rather than relative and volatile liability growth would soon haunt the pension industry and prove fatal to some (i.e., bankruptcy).

The equity correction of 2000–2002 became a pension tsunami that hit financial statements with an unexpected and damaging force. The equity decline was quite deep, and pension asset growth underperformed liability growth by as much as 75% cumulative in those three years. This event led to spiraling contribution costs because of crashing funded ratios. It also caused an EPS drain because the pension assets underperformed the ROA, which was labeled as an actuarial loss. The financial damage led to credit downgrades and even solvency issues, with several companies filing for bankruptcy (e.g., airlines) because pensions tended to be the largest liability of many firms.

Corporations were begging for relief from the spiking pension contribution costs, and Congress responded with the Pension Protection Act (US Congress 2006). In the end, PPA legislation relaxed the contribution cost calculation by offering two ways to discount liabilities: (1) a 24-month moving average of a three-segment yield curve or (2) a current spot-rate yield curve. In both options, the yield curve is based on high-quality corporate bonds rather than the 30-year Treasury rate. In effect, the PPA raised discount rates and lowered the apparent present value of liabilities, thereby enhancing the apparent funded ratio, which lowered contribution requirements.

The FASB was also concerned that existing standards did not clearly communicate the funded status on balance sheets, so it issued Statement of

---

[1]Note that this time horizon has changed a number of times in recent history.

Financial Accounting Standards No. 158: Employers' Accounting for Defined Benefit Pension and Other Postretirement Plans (Financial Accounting Standards Board 2006), effective 2007. FAS 158 clarified that the discount rates used should equal the current market value of a portfolio of high-quality zero-coupon bonds whose maturity dates and amounts matched the expected future benefit payments. This accounting standard also introduced OPEB (other postemployment benefits) liabilities onto the balance sheets as one of the largest liabilities facing US institutions.

ALM Strategies Reborn as LDI

After the 2000–03 equity correction, the stage was set to return to the basic concept of asset/liability management because of deteriorating funded ratios, large actuarial losses, and spiking contribution costs. At this time, ALM was more frequently referred to as LDI to suggest a new, enhanced approach. Some argued that there was no incentive to overfund a pension plan. Moreover, they proclaimed that there was no place for equities in a pension asset allocation. Sooner or later, they suggested, equity-based investment strategies lead to large funding shortfalls and the inability of most plan sponsors to close them.

Because of the continuing secular trend toward lower rates and the ROA accounting methodology for pension expense, however, corporations continued to pursue an asset allocation away from bonds, but this time with less equity concentration. This environment opened the asset allocation door to many new asset classes and strategies (hedge funds, alternative investments, 130–30, and so on) and new LDI strategies.

The Society of Actuaries (SOA) noticed this asset/liability disparity resulting from accounting rules and issued a research paper draft (2004) warning that accounting measures distort economic reality and produce reports inconsistent with economic results. The SOA stated further that entities that focus on economic value tend to achieve their financial objectives more consistently in the long run. In other words, the SOA promoted ALM as the proper asset management style on an economic basis (i.e., market value) and not an accounting basis.

Several prominent financial authors have advocated for the concept of "economic" values instead of accounting and actuarial valuations. Some conclude that the first element needed to manage a defined benefit plan is an "economic" view of the liability. They believe that (1) the only risks that can be hedged through investing the assets are those that are market related and (2) accounting values are not hedgeable because they are smoothed. These authors recommend that corporations align at least some of their pension assets to liabilities as the core portfolio and then add a layer of alpha on top of that. Furthermore, because the capital asset pricing model (CAPM) incorporates "economic liabilities," it thus reveals a new risk-free asset—the liability-matching asset portfolio. Many key pension experts thus promote the obvious conclusion that every corporate pension fund should be entirely in fixed-dollar investments.

A major consideration for pension assets should be the proper benchmark—one that best represents the client objective. And because the client objective is liability driven, a liability index seems to be the appropriate bogey. Each pension's liability payments are unique, so it follows that the only proper benchmark for pension assets and ALM is a custom liability index that measures the risk/reward behavior of each pension's liability schedule. Until a custom liability index is installed as the proper benchmark, all asset allocation, budget, and contribution decisions are in jeopardy.

REFERENCES

Financial Accounting Standards Board. 1985. "Statement of Financial Accounting Standards No. 87: Employers' Accounting for Pensions." FASB (December).

Financial Accounting Standards Board. 2006. "Statement of Financial Accounting Standards No. 158: Employers' Accounting for Defined Benefit Pension and Other Postretirement Plans." FASB (September).

International Association of Insurance Supervisors. 2006. "Standard on Asset-Liability Management." IAIS Standard No. 13 (October):3–6.

Society of Actuaries. 2004. "Principles Underlying Asset Liability Management." SOA Exposure Draft (October).

US Congress. 2006. "Pension Protection Act of 2006." Pub. L. 109–280, 120 Stat. 780 (www.gpo.gov/fdsys/pkg/PLAW-109publ280/pdf/PLAW-109publ280.pdf).

* * * * * *

The complete literature review, which contains 47 annotated citations on the relevant research, can be found at http://www.cfapubs.org/toc/rflr/2013/9/2.

Use your smartphone to scan the QR code to go straight to the webpage.

Fund Management: An Emotional Finance Perspective (a summary)

David Tuckett and Richard J. Taffler
Print book published 2012 and audio book published 2013
by the Research Foundation of CFA Institute
Summary prepared by David Tuckett and Richard J. Taffler

This book sets out to describe the emotional world of the fund manager. Based on more than 50 in-depth interviews with senior fund managers in the world's largest financial centres managing almost US$10 billion in assets, on average, the research asked the following questions: What is it really like being a money manager? How do money managers make sense of the highly pressurised and demanding environment in which they have to operate? How do they deal with the challenges they have to confront? And what role do their emotions play?

Conventional finance theory typically focuses on the performance of investment professionals and pays little attention to their day-to-day experiences. This important gap in our understanding of the nature of the investment process has major implications for the way financial markets work. By exploring the feelings, emotions, and experiences of real-world asset managers through interviews, we were able to construct a coherent theory of real fund management activity. The report of the findings should also help readers of the book learn from the experiences of their peers.

Emotional finance complements conventional behavioural finance, which explores the impact of cognitive biases on our investment decisions. Emotional finance formally recognises the key role our feelings and emotions, both conscious and, importantly, unconscious, play in the investment process.

Our respondents made clear that feelings and emotions play a key role in the investment task. Rather than viewing emotion as a threat to investment performance, as is often wrongly done, we show how a true understanding of the underlying emotions that drive fund manager behaviour, whether consciously acknowledged or not, is a vital component of effective decision making.

From the interviews, we could draw five main themes that are central to an understanding of the fund manager's task:

First, money managers are required to be exceptional, to outperform on a consistent basis in competition with other equally able and well-resourced fund managers. This expectation inevitably leads to emotional stress.

Second, money managers need to make decisions on the basis of a mass of incomplete, and often unreliable or conflicting, information. Investment judgements, therefore, are inevitably based on interpreting information that is inherently ambiguous in nature, which again has emotional ramifications.

Third, asset managers believe that, although market prices can diverge from fundamental value in the short term, prices converge to fundamental value in the longer term. However, because no one knows how long the convergence will take, investment decision making is based on predicting a future that is inherently uncertain.

Fourth, to be effective, fund managers believe they need to have an information advantage. They cannot know, however, whether they have an advantage or whether others are able to interpret the same information set better than they can. This ambiguity, again, leads to anxiety.

Finally, and most importantly, our interviews made clear that the relationships fund managers have with their stocks are highly emotional in nature. Even though many of our respondents claimed their competitive advantage was their ability to be emotion free, they often got carried away when talking about the stocks. They revealed that they liked and even loved stocks and managements of companies that were delivering what the mangers were hoping for and then hated the companies when they let the money managers down. Fund management is a process in which asset managers become excited in anticipation of desired future outcomes and then disappointed when things don't work out. Fund managers' feelings about their stocks are strong and volatile.

We believe that these five dimensions of the asset management task are experienced by any investment professional. In our book, we illustrate how these themes may combine and create feelings of emotional conflict and how coping with these situations is at the heart of what investment professionals have to do.

We believe that professional money managers will find that what we report from our interviews resonates with their own experiences and reveals the practical issues they face in decision making. Importantly, drawing on the insights of emotional finance, we provide a language that allows readers to talk about their own experiences and to understand the pressures under which they have to operate.

Lessons that can be learnt from this book include the recognition that all fund managers' relationships with their investments generate emotional ambivalence. This finding has implications for, for example, how to deal with buying, selling, and holding stocks when the market is going against them. We illustrate the lesson that stress and the continuous pressure by clients (and often by employers) to perform both in the short term and the

Fund Management: An Emotional Finance Perspective (a summary)

long term, irrespective of the stated mandate, are dysfunctional and not conducive to reflective analysis. We describe some of the practical ways our respondents deal with the conflicting demands placed on them and their associated high levels of anxiety. One of the clear findings is the key role a facilitative managerial environment can play in helping asset managers do their job effectively.

One of the most interesting findings of our research is how fund managers generate the conviction to act, keep their nerve, and deal with stocks that underperform by using investment 'narratives' or telling stories in various ways. The stories allow the fund managers to believe that future outcomes are predictable, leading to the commitment to act. Interestingly our quantitative managers used stories in exactly the same way as their more traditional stock-picking colleagues.

We discuss how the characteristics of the *real* risks money managers experience and are concerned about are very different from conventional statistical measures of risk used in the finance literature. The real risks to their performance generates strong emotions that are not generally recognised. Becoming aware of such feelings can help fund managers deal with the uncertainty and lack of predictability about future outcomes that they continually face. We show how the money managers we interviewed deal with real risk in their investments and portfolios.

The final chapter of the book draws on the insights of emotional finance to help us understand the characteristics of the fund manager's task. We demonstrate that the conventional distinction between rational and irrational behaviour is not meaningful and should be abandoned. All investment decision making involves emotion and intuition. Avoiding acknowledging these realities leads to a repressed state of mind.

Building on this insight, we point out how characterising investment as being about 'greed, fear, and hope', as is done conventionally, is wrong. Based on the experiences of the fund managers we interviewed, what really characterises money management is 'excitement, anxiety, and denial'. Not recognising this distinction can only lead to even more dysfunctional investment processes.

Fund management is invariably a highly emotional activity. It is driven not by conscious feelings alone but also by unconscious drives of which we are not directly aware. These feelings and drives are highly influential in determining investment behaviour. This emotional context has major implications for the nature of the asset management industry and the basis on which it operates. We conclude by arguing that an understanding of this context can lead to a more realistic view of the role of the fund manager, better comprehension of the asset management industry generally,

Research Foundations Year in Review 2013

and an appreciation of money management's real contribution in enhancing client welfare.

* * * * * *

The complete monograph can be found at http://www.cfapubs.org/toc/rf/2012/2012/2.

Use your smartphone to scan the QR code to go straight to the webpage.

"The Great Confusion: Reflections on Mean–Variance Optimization" with Harry Markowitz (a summary)

Summary prepared by Nathan Erickson, CFA

The Nobel Prize in Economics is an award for outstanding contributions to the field, and it is generally regarded as the most prestigious award in economics. In 1990, the award was given to three men recognized as pioneers in the theory of financial economics and corporate finance: Merton Miller, for his fundamental contributions to the theory of corporate finance; William Sharpe, for his contributions to the theory of price formation for financial assets, called the "capital asset pricing model" (CAPM); and Harry Markowitz, for having developed the theory of portfolio choice, called "mean–variance optimization."

It is rare in one's profession to be able to spend time with a pioneer. On 8 May 2013, Markowitz conducted a live webinar co-sponsored by CFA Society Tucson and CFA Society Phoenix and supported by CFA Institute and the Research Foundation of CFA Institute. The title of the discussion was "The Great Confusion: Reflections on Mean–Variance Optimization."

Mean–variance optimization is the basis of modern portfolio theory and the method for building diversified portfolios that maximizes return for a given level of risk. Markowitz developed the concept in the 1950s. Since 2008, there has been much debate about mean–variance optimization and whether it protected investors adequately during the market crisis.

Even at the age of 85, Markowitz continues to conduct significant research in the field and is regularly published in academic journals. In the webinar, we discussed some of his research regarding alternative methods to calculate risk, which some have suggested are necessary to improve mean–variance optimization. His conclusion, which will be published in a forthcoming book, is that adjustments to account for risks not captured by the normal or log-normal distribution are not necessary and that the original components of mean–variance optimization are sufficient to build optimal portfolios that perform as expected during any market environment. He also reiterated that mean–variance optimization *did* work in 2008: A portfolio diversified across asset classes performed better than an all-equity portfolio. In times of market crises, when assets all go down together—and such events do occur—the investor's risk tolerance needs to be reassessed.

Markowitz went into great detail on a number of academic points, and near the end of the webinar, he shifted to more of the art of portfolio management and its application in today's world. This section includes his comments on behavioral finance, the implications of quantitative easing and regulatory changes on portfolio construction, the impact of high-frequency trading, whether investors should have a "home bias," and how to determine appropriate asset classes and constraints.

To conclude our webinar, Markowitz provided two excellent quotes. The first relates to the art of mean–variance optimization: "In the right hands, mean–variance analysis is as flexible as a set of oil colors in the hands of Picasso, Van Gogh, or Rembrandt, and in the wrong hands, it's just paint by numbers and you don't know what you're going to get." Finally, with regard to investing in general and dealing with all of the unknown variables, he shared advice he was given by a professor when he was young: "Don't ask, 'What do I know?' Ask, 'How should I act?'"

* * * * * *

Video of the entire presentation can be found at http://www.cfainstitute.org/learning/foundation/research/Pages/multimedia.aspx.

Use your smartphone to scan the QR code to go straight to the webpage.

Who Should Hedge Tail Risk? (a summary)

Robert Litterman
Presentation at the 12th Annual Research for the Practitioner Workshop, 19 May 2013
Summary prepared by Bud Haslett, CFA, and Laurence B. Siegel

My first exposure to hedging tail risk began 20 years ago when, as a partner at Goldman Sachs, I was asked to examine hedging the partnership's risk in case of a stock market crash. The decision at that time was to contact the equity derivatives department and put on a tail risk hedge. The position was implemented and examined after being in place for about a year, and the hedge was found to be the worst of all worlds because of the high cost of hedging and the small level of protection it provided (only about 10% of the value of the firm). The partners decided that this hedge did not make any sense.

Fast forward to the financial crisis of 2008–2009. The lesson of the crisis for many investors was that they really need to hedge the tail risk. The problem is the price of the hedge can be prohibitive. Given my past experience with hedging tail risk, I asked myself, does it really make sense? If everyone hedges tail risk, who will sell the protection? And ultimately, who should be buying and who should be selling tail risk insurance?

For tail risk insurance that pays off when financial markets have dropped substantially, the natural buyers are those who are hurt more when financial markets are down, such as

- leveraged financial institutions,
- those with less liquidity,
- those with short time horizons,
- hedge funds,
- market makers, and
- banks.

The natural sellers of tail risk insurance are those financial institutions that have less exposure to an economic downturn, for example

- long-term investors,

- investors who do not use leverage, and
- those with significant liquidity.

These natural sellers include pensions, sovereign wealth funds, endowments, and insurance companies.

Many of the firms that were seeking to buy tail risk insurance following the crisis were those that should have been natural sellers of tail risk. Why were they seeking to buy the insurance in the first place? This desire is a natural response to having just gone through a crisis, but the reason to buy tail risk insurance may be a behavioral issue rooted in the belief that you can take more risk as long as you have some protection from extreme events. One way to determine if you should buy tail risk insurance is to ask yourself these five questions:

1. Am I a natural buyer or a natural seller?
2. Is today's price of tail risk high enough to make it too unattractive for me as a buyer?
3. Is my risk exposure basically a linear function of the amount of equities I hold? (If so, you can just hold less in equities to reduce risk; if the risk increases faster than the equity allocation, you may want to hedge.)
4. If my equity exposure is too large, is there a less expensive way to reduce my equity risk?
5. Is the governance structure of the fund leading management to consider buying tail risk insurance in order to protect itself, even if such a purchase is not in the fund beneficiaries' long-term interest?

The primary reason tail risk is so expensive is fairly obvious: Tail risk insurance pays off in bad times, when money is most valuable, which is the opposite of what equities do; they pay off in good times, when the value of an additional dollar is lowest. Equities deliver a risk premium, whereas tail risk insurance charges a risk premium. Two additional reasons explain the high price of tail risk insurance:

- The seller of tail risk insurance sacrifices much of the upside from the equity risk premium while retaining the full downside.
- As Antti Ilmanen found in "Do Financial Markets Reward Buying or Selling Insurance and Lottery Tickets?" the market places a premium on both lottery tickets and insurance. That is, extreme or tail events are very expensive to bet on. This, Ilmanen believes, is a behavioral phenomenon caused by natural demand from investors.[1]

---

[1]Antti Ilmanen, "Do Financial Markets Reward Buying or Selling Insurance and Lottery Tickets?" *Financial Analysts Journal*, vol. 68, no. 5 (September/October 2012):26–36.

Let's look at the return from tail risk hedging. The basic hedging instrument is the VXX, an exchange-traded note (ETN) that represents a continuous, rolled-over investment in VIX (an equity volatility index) futures. The return on the VXX is thus the return from buying insurance on the equity market. The S&P 500 Index and the VXX are negatively correlated, so the insurance "works" during periods of negative equity return. But over time, the tail risk insurance loses a lot of money. In the financial crisis of 2008–2009, for example, the market crashed but then recovered nicely. The VXX, however, which started at 100 and later went to 200, went down to about 2, so investors lost 98% of their original investment, or 99% from the peak. This loss in the long term offsets some of the gain from tail risk hedging in bad periods and may be regarded as the cost of having hedged.

So, is paying a premium to get insurance the best way to reduce the risk of your portfolio? There are three strategies for reducing equity exposure:

Strategy 1: Buy tail risk insurance (the S&P 500 plus 10% exposure in the VXX).

Strategy 2: Sell equity (hold 75% in equity and 25% in Treasury bills).

Strategy 3: Sell more equity and sell tail risk insurance (hold 50% in the S&P 500 and 50% in Treasury bills while selling tail risk insurance on 10% of the portfolio).

A comparison of the results from these strategies for 2006–2013 shows that Strategy 1 cut off the lower tail but cost a lot in the end. Strategy 2 also reduced risk and had a return similar to that of the all-equity strategy (because stocks and Treasury bills had similar returns over the period studied). Strategy 3 had the best return.

During the crisis, all three of these strategies provided some benefit. The S&P 500 was down 47% during the crisis (1 March 2008 to 2 March 2009). So, buying 10% tail risk (Strategy 1) caused you to be down 39.7%. You got similar results if you cut equity exposure to 75% (Strategy 2); you were down 36%. The final strategy caused you to be down 34%.

These strategies were all effective at reducing losses and volatility, but over the full sample, 2006–2013, a 100% equity portfolio had a compound annual return of 3.5%. Thus, holding 100% equities and buying tail risk on 10% of the portfolio (Strategy 1) returned 0.8%; holding 75% in equities (Strategy 2) returned 3.5%; and holding 50% in equities and selling tail risk on 10% of the portfolio (Strategy 3) returned 5.9%. This last return includes the premium earned from selling tail risk. The Sharpe ratios of the strategies tell a similar story.

What is the bottom line? Should you buy tail risk insurance? Natural buyers of tail risk insurance—for example, investment banks—should go to natural sellers, such as pension funds, to try to sell them this insurance. But natural sellers should not buy it; they should ask investment banks to make a two-sided market in tail risk insurance so they can sell it instead.

* * * * * *

Video of the entire presentation can be found at http://www.cfainstitute.org/learning/products/multimedia/Pages/88139.aspx.

Use your smartphone to scan the QR code to go straight to the webpage.

Specifying and Managing Tail Risk in Multi-Asset Portfolios (a summary)

Pranay Gupta, CFA
Presentation at the 12th Annual Research for the
Practitioner Workshop, 19 May 2013
Summary prepared by Pranay Gupta, CFA

One of the most prominent problems in multi-asset portfolio management is the management of tail risk, which arises at each step in the investment process. In general, all multi-asset investment processes follow three steps, each of which contributes to overall tail risk and each of which raises a question:

1. *allocating assets or risk into buckets*—can we design a multi-asset allocation process that helps minimize tail risk?

2. *selecting strategies*, active or passive, to fulfill the allocation chosen—at what level of underperformance should one liquidate an underperforming manager?

3. *selecting securities within each investment strategy*—can we design a portfolio construction process to manage the tail contribution from each asset?

This presentation proposes improved methodologies for Steps 1 and 3.

Individual Asset Classes

Eight common liquid asset classes are used in most allocation processes: equities (US, European, Japanese, and Asian), fixed income (sovereigns, credits, and high yield), and gold, which is used more commonly in wealth management than commodities. For the moment, I have excluded both alternative and illiquid assets.

Each of these individual asset classes has poor tail risk characteristics. As an example, from 2000 to 2012, all equity asset classes had maximum drawdowns of more than 50%, fixed-income asset classes had a drawdown of 33%, and gold, 26%. Sovereigns had a maximum drawdown of only 4%, but this number arguably might have been much larger over a full interest rate cycle. Furthermore, diversification benefits are in reality quite minimal because correlations between the equity asset classes (including high yield because it has equity-like behavior) averaged more than 80% recently and those between fixed-income instruments (ex credit risk) were around 93% over this period.

Thus, the asset allocation process devolves from allocating to eight asset classes to allocating only to two (equities and credits). Effectively, the investor has to try to time the market, which we know cannot be done sustainably with skill. Even with a full look-ahead portfolio (i.e., perfect investment skill), if an investor had invested in the two top-performing asset classes, with quarterly rebalancing, the portfolio would have incurred a maximum drawdown of –12% at a 10% confidence level in this period.

This level of drawdown is more than what asset owners expect, given the average asset class premium earned—hence the need for an improved asset allocation and tail risk management process.

Improved Allocation Framework

The ubiquitous approach followed in multi-asset investing is to have a single allocation process that allocates assets or risk to specified buckets. Alpha risk is then diversified by deploying a large number of managers. This is odd because in any multi-asset portfolio, the majority of portfolio risk and return comes from the beta allocation decision, not the alpha decision. I would, therefore, argue that a better portfolio results from following a multi-strategy approach to asset allocation. For instance, Gupta and Straatman (2006) show that using a multi-strategy investment process can create strategy diversification and decrease portfolio risk. The same concept is applied here to the allocation process. In multi-asset investing, the allocation processes are grouped into five main categories:

1. *economic view based*—traditional macro view–based forecasting of asset markets.
2. *risk based*—including risk parity, minimum variance, and risk budgeting.
3. *fundamental systematic*—economic/fundamental weighted, thematic, and factor-based approaches.
4. *long-term risk premium*—long-term studies, as well as balanced and target date strategies.
5. *alpha only*—shorter-term strategies, such as macro hedge funds, commodity trading advisers, and managed futures.

By incorporating all five types of allocation processes in a portfolio, strategy risk is decreased. And because these processes have different biases as to when they are effective and when they are not, an additional strategy allocation layer can enable tilting the portfolio toward the style in vogue.

Although seemingly a logical and simple concept, this allocation approach has dramatic implications for the asset management structure:

- Plan sponsors will need to modify their allocation structure by having multiple allocation groups, each using a different process of allocating assets, which are then invested appropriately.

- The debate surrounding the superiority of asset allocation versus risk allocation can be resolved because both can co-exist in the same portfolio, with each part working to a different degree of efficacy at different points in the market cycle.

- The choice of buckets (asset classes, geographical areas, or factors) can also be made such that all can co-exist because the bucket choice is determined by each allocation method independently.

Furthermore, using all five allocation processes enables the allocation to be made at different investment horizons within the same portfolio, which, as detailed later, allows us to manage tail risk considerably better.

Redefining Tail Risk

Conventional literature often uses the end-of-horizon asset return distribution to measure tail risk. In practice, however, the governance structure of all asset owners and asset managers forces the review of performance periodically within the investment horizon. Thus, I propose that tail risk should not be measured using only an end-of-horizon estimation but should be a composite of two drawdown risks:

- *end-of-horizon risk*—the probability of the target return not being met at the end of the investment horizon, and

- *intra-horizon risk*—the probability of breaching a given maximum drawdown threshold at any time within the investment horizon.

Using such a composite represents portfolio risk more accurately and is more likely to lead to a portfolio that does not suffer unexpected outcomes, as compared with using only an end-of-horizon risk estimation.

Impact of a Long-Term Investment Horizon

A standard lognormal process can be used to model a portfolio construction process. Defined parameters include the universe from which assets can be selected as well as the investment process (or manager) Sharpe ratio. Parameters that can be chosen by the portfolio manager are the number of assets in the portfolio and their volatilities, the investment horizon of each asset, and the stop loss imposed for each asset.

The parameterized model concludes that end-of-horizon risk decreases as investment horizon increases. This finding substantiates conventional logic as to why one should have a long investment horizon: You are more likely to reach your desired investment objective in the long run.

At the same time, intra-horizon risk increases quite dramatically as investment horizon increases. That is, if an investor chooses a longer horizon as advocated, the investor is more likely to breach the tolerance for maximum drawdown at some point during the investment horizon.

If an investor truly did not want to observe mark-to-market returns periodically, or was unable to observe them (as with illiquid investments), then a long-term investment horizon would indeed make sense. In practice, however, because performance reviews are possible at any time, it might not be appropriate for all asset owners to have a long-term investment horizon. Instead, a portfolio's optimal investment horizon should be determined based on the asset owner's tolerance threshold for intra-horizon risk.

Using Investment Horizon to Manage Tail Risk

The standard model can be extended to incorporate uncertainty about the mean return, similar to the Black–Litterman model (1992). But doing so has nontrivial implications because the standard deviation no longer grows with the square root of time and the Sharpe ratio is no longer time homogenous.

Although the basic result of tail risk increasing as return uncertainty increases is an expected one, this framework can then be used to construct a portfolio that explicitly incorporates the asset owner's intra-horizon risk aversion. Specifically, the portfolio manager can choose the combination of investment horizon and uncertainty of expected return (skill) for each asset so as to stay within intra-horizon risk limits. It then follows that for a given maximum intra-horizon risk threshold, long-term fundamental managers need to be much more certain of their skill compared with short-term traders.

Defining Optimal Stop-Loss Levels

A portfolio manager buys stocks in a portfolio based on positive expected return. A stock is replaced when the target return is reached, or when a maximum holding period is reached, or when the stock hits a defined stop-loss level. The question thus arises that given a maximum drawdown threshold for the overall portfolio, can customized stop-loss levels be defined for each stock based on its individual characteristics? If the stop loss is set too tight, increased transaction costs will negatively affect portfolio return, and if set too loose, large drawdowns may occur.

The parameterized model is used to determine the impact of implementing varying stop-loss levels on different portfolio assets. Results show that stop-loss levels need to be tighter when mean uncertainty increases, investment horizons are longer, and transaction costs are lower. This finding then leads to a framework that can be applied to determine optimal stop losses at the asset level and to a framework that can be aligned with the asset owner's tolerance threshold for intra-horizon drawdown. This approach can be used for stocks in a stock portfolio, asset classes in a multi-asset portfolio, or strategies in a fund of managers.

Conclusion

Constructing a multi-asset portfolio with a constraint of tail risk aversion is challenging because (1) the individual asset classes have poor tail risk characteristics and (2) diversification between asset classes is minimal. A better portfolio can be achieved using a multi-strategy framework for the allocation process, whereby different methods of asset and risk allocation co-exist as independent strategies within the same portfolio. This framework creates strategy diversification, allows allocation to be done at multiple investment horizons, and helps to manage tail risk of the portfolio.

Conventional tail risk measures, which use only the end-of-horizon return distribution, fail to capture the real risk that an asset owner has of intra-horizon drawdown. Thus, a tail risk measure that is a composite of intra-horizon and end-of-horizon risk should lead to a portfolio with fewer unexpected outcomes.

Finally, a better and more aligned portfolio is created if intra-horizon risk is incorporated into the portfolio construction process, the investment horizon of each asset in the portfolio is chosen, and customized stop-loss levels are implemented at the asset level.

Bibliography

Black, Fischer, and Robert Litterman. 1992. "Global Portfolio Optimization." *Financial Analysts Journal*, vol. 48, no. 5 (September/October):28–43.

Grossman, Sanford, and Zhongquan Zhou. 1993. "Optimal Investment Strategies for Controlling Drawdowns." *Mathematical Finance*, vol. 3, no. 3 (July):241–276.

Gupta, Pranay, and Sven Skallsjö. 2013. "Rethinking the Asset Allocation Approach for Plan Sponsors." Working paper (http://ssrn.com/abstract=2210695).

———. 2013. "Specifying and Managing Tail Risk in Portfolios—A Practical Approach." Working paper (http://ssrn.com/abstract=2270914).

Gupta, Pranay, and Jan Straatman. 2006. "Skill-Based Investment Management." *Journal of Investment Management*, vol. 4, no. 1 (First Quarter):1–18.

Magdon-Ismail, Malik, Amir F. Atiya, Amrit Pratap, and Yaser S. Abu-Mostafa. 2004. "On the Maximum Drawdown of a Brownian Motion." *Journal of Applied Probability*, vol. 41, no. 1 (March):147–161.

Pástor, Ľuboš, and Robert F. Stambaugh. 2012. "Are Stocks Really Less Volatile in the Long Run?" *Journal of Finance*, vol. 67, no. 2 (April):431–478.

James R. Vertin Award

The James R. Vertin Award is presented periodically to recognize individuals who have produced a body of research notable for its relevance and enduring value to investment professionals. This award was established in 1996 to honor James R. Vertin, CFA, for his outstanding leadership in promoting excellence and relevancy in research and education.

2013 Vertin Award Winners

Richard C. Grinold

Richard C. Grinold is a founding director and member of the advisory council of Vinva Investment Management in Sydney, Australia. Before joining Vinva, he served as the global director of research at Barclays Global Investors (BGI). The group was responsible for active investment strategies of US$240 billion invested in equity, fixed-income, and global macro asset allocation strategies. Prior to his work at BGI, he was director of research and later president of BARRA, a leading global investment technology company.

Richard spent 20 years on the faculty of the School of Business Administration at the University of California, Berkeley. At UC Berkeley Richard served, at various times, as chair of the finance faculty, chair of the management science faculty, and director of the Berkeley Program in Finance. He left UC Berkeley in early 1989 to devote full time to his work at BARRA. Richard also served as a research fellow at Harvard University in 1968–69, a fellow at the Center for Operations Research and Econometrics (CORE) in Belgium in 1974, a visiting professor at HEC Paris in 1979–1980, and a visiting professor at the Harvard Business School in 1983–1984.

Richard received his PhD in operations research from UC Berkeley in 1968. He studied physics at Tufts University and helped to wire up the Cambridge Electron Accelerator. Other milestones include serving as the navigator of the USS *Gainard*.

Ronald N. Kahn

Ronald N. Kahn is a managing director and the Global Head of Scientific Equity Research at BlackRock. He is responsible for upholding and enhancing BlackRock's scientific equity research standards and products. Ron's service with the firm dates back to 1998, including his years with BGI, which merged with BlackRock in 2009. At BGI, his roles included global head of equity research, global head of advanced equity strategies, and head of active equities in the United States. Prior to joining BGI, Ron worked as director of research at BARRA, where his research covered equity and fixed-income markets in the United States and globally.

With Richard Grinold, Ron authored *Active Portfolio Management: Quantitative Theory and Applications*. He is a 2007 winner of the Bernstein Fabozzi/Jacobs Levy Award for best article in the *Journal of Portfolio Management*. He serves on the editorial advisory boards of the *Financial Analysts Journal*, the *Journal of Portfolio Management*, and the *Journal of Investment Consulting*. Ron teaches the equities half of the course "International Equity and Currency Markets" in UC Berkeley's Master of Financial Engineering Program.

Ron earned an AB degree in physics, summa cum laude, from Princeton University in 1978 and a PhD in physics from Harvard University in 1985. He was also a post-doctoral fellow in physics at the University of California, Berkeley.

Past Vertin Award Winners

2012 Elroy Dimson
2010 Roger Clarke
2009 Robert Shiller
2008 Keith Ambachtsheer
2007 Campbell R. Harvey
2006 Clifford S. Asness
2005 Andrew W. Lo
2004 Edwin J. Elton
2004 Martin Gruber

2003 Barr Rosenberg
2002 William L. Fouse, CFA
2001 Rex A. Sinquefield
2001 Roger G. Ibbotson
2000 Peter L. Bernstein
1998 Martin L. Leibowitz
1997 Jack L. Treynor
1996 William F. Sharpe

Evolving into the Science of Investing: Presentation upon Receiving the James R. Vertin Award

Ronald N. Kahn

I want to start by thanking the Research Foundation of CFA Institute for awarding Richard Grinold and me the James R. Vertin Award. It is a great honor. I also want to thank Richard Grinold—mentor, manager, colleague, and co-author—for taking a chance back in 1987 and hiring a physics PhD with no knowledge of finance. What an adventure this has been.

In 2000, Richard Grinold and I started our book *Active Portfolio Management* by stating:

> The art of investing is evolving into the science of investing. This evolution has been happening slowly and will continue for some time. . . . As new generations of increasingly scientific investment managers come to the task, they will rely more on analysis, process, and structure than on intuition, advice, and whim. (p. 1)

So, how has this evolution into the science of investing been going? How much progress have we made? My perspective on this is different today in 2013 from what it was in 2006.

To investigate this question, let's start by reviewing some of the prior research on the adoption of new (non-investment) technology. Individuals and institutions adopt new technology based on a cost–benefit analysis under uncertainty and with limited information. The decision is often less about whether to adopt a new technology than about whether to adopt it now or later.

The speed of adoption depends on the details of that cost–benefit analysis and how it changes over time. If we focus on organizations that are either creating new technology or deciding to use new technology, the cost analysis includes the costs of developing or acquiring and implementing the technology. Part of the costs will cover education and training, especially if the skill level required for the new technology is high. The benefit analysis will cover the added value of the new technology, which can vary over time because of network effects. Many technologies (e.g., fax machines and e-mail) become more valuable as they are more widely used.

New technology adoption typically follows S-shaped curves over time. Initially, we see a small number of early adopters. Then, successful technologies experience more rapid adoption. Finally, adoption saturates as the set of potential adopters dwindles. **Figure 1** shows these adoption curves for selected consumer products.

Research Foundation Year in Review 2013

Figure 1. Diffusion Rates in the United States for Selected Consumer Products

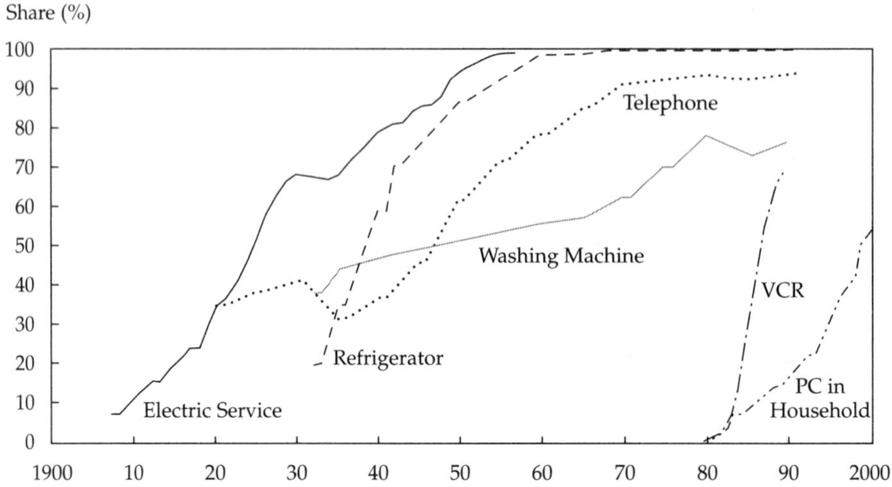

[Chart showing diffusion rates from 1900 to 2000 for: Electric Service, Refrigerator, Washing Machine, Telephone, VCR, and PC in Household. Y-axis: Share (%) from 0 to 100.]

Source: Hall and Khan (2003).

The figure shows that refrigerators and VCRs experienced very rapid adoption in the United States, whereas washing machines and electric service were adopted more slowly. Eventually, nearly the entire United States adopted electric service and refrigerators, but perhaps 25% of the population still has not adopted washing machines (presumably, most of these people use washing machines at laundromats).

Now, let's look at three examples in the world of investing: equity indexing, equity risk modeling, and quantitative active equity strategies. All of these fall under the general rubric of scientific investing. In each case, I will consider adoption in the context of this model of technology adoption.

Equity Indexing

The idea for equity indexing goes back to 1964, when Sharpe developed the CAPM.[1] In 1974, Black and Scholes published a paper describing initial attempts to build such a product:

> The modern theory of finance suggests that most investors should put part or all of their money into a "market portfolio." . . . Attempts to create a fund based on these principles and to make it available to a large number of investors have uncovered some important problems. Legal costs due to government regulations, the costs of managing a fund, and especially the costs of selling

[1] Treynor (1961), Lintner (1965), and Mossin (1966) were on roughly the same track in the same era.

Evolving into the Science of Investing

it are all much higher than one might expect. *Despite these problems, efforts to create such funds seem destined for eventual success.* (italics added, p. 399)

Black and Scholes were certainly correct in their forecast that index funds would eventually succeed. But the costs of developing indexing were high, as they describe in the quote. The level of financial modeling skill required in developing these products was quite high relative to standards at that time. Education was a particular challenge, especially educating potential investors on the advantages of being average! The benefits become clear only after significant education. In the case of indexing, there was no particular network effect. The benefits of indexing exist for the first adopter and do not particularly increase with the number of adopters.

Remarkably, the Wells Fargo Investment Advisors equity index product, the first index fund, was unprofitable for its first 13 years. Today, indexing is a huge and profitable business. As an interesting aside for this occasion, James R. Vertin played a central role in Wells Fargo's pioneering efforts to develop index funds.

As for maximum adoption, we expect equity indexing to saturate at less than 100%. In spite of the many benefits of indexing, we do not expect 100% of assets to be indexed. If that were to happen, it would threaten price discovery.

So, what has been the history of adoption of equity indexing? **Figure 2** shows US institutional indexed equity assets under management (AUM) from the early 1970s through 2007.

From 1971 through 1983, total AUM was less than $15 billion, crossing $1 trillion in 1997. Although Figure 2 does not display the typical S-curve

Figure 2. US Institutional Indexed Equity Assets under Management

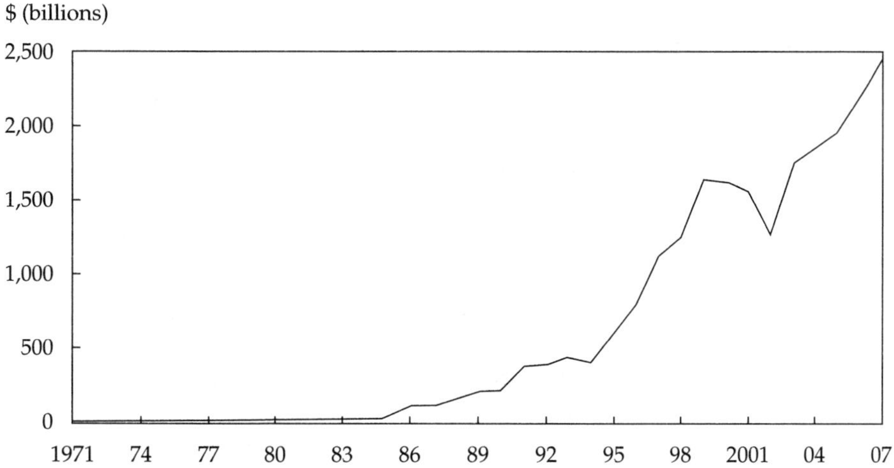

Source: PricewaterhouseCoopers, *Pensions & Investments*.

shape, based on the time required to cross $1 trillion, we can surmise that adoption of equity indexing required about 25 years.

Equity Risk Modeling

The ideas underlying equity risk modeling go back to Markowitz (1959), Sharpe (1963), and Rosenberg (1974). By the mid-1970s, Barra equity risk models were commercially available. Interestingly, the National Science Foundation funded their initial development. As with indexing, risk models required a high level of financial modeling skill—both to develop and to use—compared with the standards at that time. As to the benefits of risk modeling, they become quite obvious after big losses arising from poor risk management. There has been a network effect associated with risk models, at least in some applications. For example, Barra model output became a standard requirement to receive quotes for trading baskets of stocks.

Risk models were not immediately adopted. A drawing of Barr Rosenberg appeared on the cover of *Institutional Investor* magazine in 1978 under the headline "Who is Barr Rosenberg, and what the hell is he talking about?" The illustration showed Rosenberg in the lotus position, seated on a prayer rug, with flowers in his hair, and with a group of much smaller money managers in suits bowing down to him. Charitably, we can call that the "age of early adopters" for equity risk models.

Although I do not have a graph of the growth of assets managed using risk models, I suspect the vast majority of assets are now in products managed in part by using risk model analysis. Risk modeling should saturate at near 100% because all investors benefit from understanding the risks in their portfolios. So, like for equity indexing, adoption has taken about 25 years.

Quantitative Equity Investing

Quantitative equity investing applies rigorous and systematic analysis (i.e., the scientific method) to develop return forecasts. It views investing as a mathematical optimization problem, trading off expected return against risk and cost. Quantitative equity strategies are designed to maximize consistency of positive returns—that is, the *information ratio* (ratio of active return to risk). This is a philosophy of investing, not a specific strategy like investing based on book-to-price ratios or price momentum.

Quantitative equity strategies began in the late 1970s and early 1980s, when some financial economists began identifying persistent mispricings and applying quantitative approaches to forecasting equity returns.

Quantitative equity strategies are costly to develop and continually improve. And success requires continuous improvement; ideas stop working as markets understand them. (There are no beneficial network effects in active management, only detrimental network effects.) Quantitative equity strategies require high levels of financial modeling skill and, critically, a nose for great investment ideas. They also involve significant costs to educate clients as to their benefits. As with all active strategies, signal-to-noise ratios are low. Convincing clients to adopt these strategies requires education and time.

With all that as background, the history of adoption of these strategies has been quite mixed, as **Figure 3** demonstrates.

Figure 3 shows indicative levels of assets invested in quantitative equity strategies, based on US SEC 13F filings of firms exclusively following quantitative equity strategies. This figure is an underestimate of the true AUM invested in these strategies because it ignores firms that offer a wide range of investment styles, but it is indicative of the pattern of investing in these strategies.

Quantitative equity strategies began in the late 1970s and early 1980s, but Figure 3 starts in 1997. As you can see, quantitative equity strategies experienced a large growth spurt from 2003 through the middle of 2007, after which they declined very quickly. This is a pattern we would not expect to see with indexing or risk modeling, but it is one that can be seen with active investing. By 2007, too much money had flowed into these strategies. The sub-prime mortgage crisis required many investors to raise capital to meet margin requirements. Rather

Figure 3. Indicative Quant Assets under Management from 13F Filings

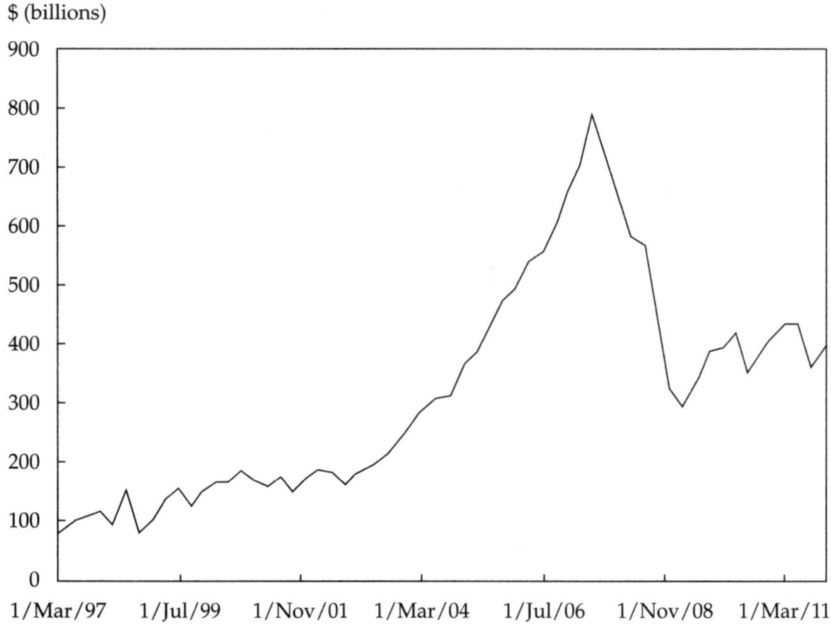

Source: BlackRock.

than sell illiquid sub-prime mortgages, many investors withdrew funds from the much more liquid quantitative equity strategies. Unfortunately, most quantitative equity managers followed similar strategies and hence held correlated positions, which led to very volatile performance in August 2007, followed by more leisurely paced withdrawals over the following two years. It is estimated that quantitative equity investments are now down 75% from their peak in mid-2007.

Continued Evolution into the Science of Investing

If I were giving this talk in 2006, the evolution into the science of investing would be looking very positive. Equity indexing was already widespread in 2006, as were equity risk models. And quantitative equity strategies had experienced significant growth. The perspective from 2013 is not quite as rosy, given the significant drop in quantitative equity strategies.

There are some reasons to be pessimistic about this evolution. During the financial crisis, a senior investment professional (not a scientific investor) commented to me, "Don't these quant things blow up every five years or so?" This sophisticated professional had lumped together quantitative equity strategies, portfolio insurance, Long-Term Capital Management, mortgage derivatives—basically every investment idea over the past 25 years that involved college-level math. The education effort still has far to go.

Another investor, a pioneering academic turned investment professional, told me, "We were lucky to have lived during the golden age of financial innovation. But now it's over." So, even some scientific investors are pessimistic about this evolution into the science of investing.

But I am optimistic that the evolution will continue, for three reasons.

First, the world has already changed. Indexing is very well established, as are equity risk models. And if too many assets flowed into quantitative equity strategies, not all have left. Asset levels have stabilized and even started to grow again. The optimal saturation point is somewhere between current levels and the highs of 2007. We should never have expected that the adoption of quantitative equity strategies would come close to the adoption of indexing. Beyond these strategies, investments in many different asset classes are increasingly managed in part with scientific ideas.

Second, clients are in critical need of innovation and improvements in asset management. Unfortunately, the world is full of examples of underfunded pension plans and poorly managed investments.

Third, the scientific method has won out in most fields of human endeavor. Why should investing be different? I have to believe that rigor and analysis are on the right side of history. The Research Foundation and CFA Institute believe that as well.

Thank you.

References

Black, Fischer, and Myron S. Scholes. 1974. "From Theory to a New Financial Product." *Journal of Finance*, vol. 29, no. 2 (May):399–412.

Grinold, Richard C., and Ronald N. Kahn. 2000. *Active Portfolio Management.* 2nd ed. New York: McGraw-Hill.

Hall, Bronwyn, and Beethika Khan. 2003. "Adoption of New Technology." In *New Economy Handbook*. Edited by Derek C. Jones. San Diego, CA: Academic Press.

Lintner, John. 1965. "The Valuation of Risky Assets and the Selection of Risky Investments in Stock Portfolios and Capital Budgets." *Review of Economics and Statistics*, vol. 47, no. 1 (February):13–37.

Markowitz, H. 1959. *Portfolio Selection: Efficient Diversification of Investment.* Cowles Foundation Monograph 16. New Haven, CT: Yale University Press.

Mossin, Jan. 1966. "Equilibrium in a Capital Asset Market." *Econometrica*, vol. 34, no. 4 (October):768–783.

Rosenberg, B. 1974. "Extra-Market Components of Covariance in Security Markets." *Journal of Financial and Quantitative Analysis*, vol. 9, no. 2 (March):263–274.

Sharpe, William F. 1963. "A Simplified Model for Portfolio Analysis." *Management Science*, vol. 9, no. 2 (January):277–293.

———. 1964. "Capital Asset Prices: A Theory of Market Equilibrium under Conditions of Risk." *Journal of Finance*, vol. 19, no. 3 (September):425–442.

Treynor, J.L. 1961. "Toward a Theory of the Market Value of Risky Assets." Unpublished manuscript.

Observations from a Career in Investment Management: Presentation upon Receiving the James R. Vertin Award

Richard Grinold

Rather than give a technical talk, I'll take a personal approach and describe how I got here and some interesting things that happened along the way. The early part is not very interesting or unusual: born, grew up, went to school, college, worked for a year, Navy for 3.5 years, then graduate school. The first surprise came after graduate school, when I stayed on as a professor. This was not the plan. I thought I would get a "real" job, but something—inertia, a lack of imagination, a dearth of interesting alternatives—left me in school. After a year marking time as a post-doc, I found myself teaching management science at the University of California Berkeley's Business School; this was unexplored territory.

After I had spent four years at Berkeley, an opportunity came up to teach a finance course. I had never taken a finance course, so I accepted. In our more enlightened times, this move might have been classified as "experimenting on students without their consent." I'm not sure about the students, but I, at least, survived the experiment, and a few years later, I was allowed to teach a seminar in finance. I chose pension fund finance as the topic because I knew nothing about it. Students and professor would learn together. For a text, I selected a monograph I had not read called *The Financial Reality of Pension Funding under ERISA* by the then-editor of the *Financial Analysts Journal*, Jack Treynor.[1] I was pleasantly surprised and found the book to contain an agreeable blend of analytical insight and common sense. After I realized Treynor was also masquerading as Walter Bagehot in the pages of the *FAJ*, I started looking for more of Treynor's insights and became a regular *FAJ* reader.

Never underestimate serendipity. I was fortunate in that the fates had placed my office next to that of Barr Rosenberg. In the late 1970s, Barr asked me to consult for what was then a strange new firm called BARRA. Work at BARRA showed me many of the actual challenges faced by investment managers. Among the greatest of these challenges was the torment in preparing for and taking the CFA exam. Every June, BARRA would hold a research seminar at Pebble Beach, California. The conference started on a Sunday and

---

[1]Treynor's co-authors were Patrick J. Regan and William W. Priest.

usually on the day following the CFA exams. The survivors of these Level I, II, and III exams became the social engine of the conference and did some serious unwinding.

It was also at BARRA that I met Ronald Kahn. Ron is that rare spirit who is both extremely intelligent and unpretentious. I'm not sure how Ron found us, but we were fortunate. I do recall our first interview, in 1988, which went something like this:

>RCG: So, you studied physics at Princeton and Harvard . . . and your thesis?
>RNK: The early universe.
>RCG: Ahh . . . How early?
>RNK: The first 10 seconds.
>RCG: That is early! And what are you doing now?
>RNK: Studying the extinction of the dinosaurs.
>RCG: Ah, that's a 13-billion-year-less-10-second jump. Shouldn't be difficult to shuffle forward a mere 65 million years and get in touch with the post–Black Monday equity market.

Of course, we hired him, and it was a brilliant decision.

Work in the financial industry required skills that were complementary to the required skills found in academe. I was fortunate to have spent enough time in school to learn a few things but not enough time to get indoctrinated. I knew what the KOOL-AID looked like, but I did not sip from the cup. Although economics and finance use mathematics and statistics in the same way that the physical sciences use them, the purpose in the social sciences is to maintain the logic of an argument, to get from A to B safely and prevent sloppy thinking. This doesn't mean the results at B are useful; it just means that the steps from A to B are valid.

Nevertheless, the precision of the argument lends an aura of truth to the result—an effect that is unwarranted and often misleading. After all, finance and economics are *social* sciences. Results are guidelines; they will be, at best, sort of true most of the time. In the investment world, one hears such comments as "it was a bad year for growth stocks." As one wag has pointed out, you don't hear scientists saying "it was a bad year for gravity."

Consider the capital asset pricing model (CAPM): The vital takeaway of the CAPM for the would-be active manager is not that markets are efficient, full stop, but that the burden of proof lies heavily on anyone who has a scheme to outperform the markets. In particular, one should be suspicious of elaborate arguments in which hypotheses are compounded and results smack of wheels within wheels. I tend to like simple, even crude, models that provide a first-order relationship between important variables.

Eventually, I found myself in the world of active portfolio management. I was lucky enough to work for James Vertin's old firm, Wells Fargo Nikko Investment Advisors, which eventually morphed into Barclays Global Investors (BGI).

BGI was a wonderful place. It was crammed full of interesting and intelligent people who were motivated by two modest goals: to be the very best in the business and to revolutionize the investment management industry. They were, and they did.

Now, I am retired and seeing the industry from the outside. I occasionally meet new people, and they ask what I did. I generally reply "investment management" and get an "Oh, where?" response. I say, "Barclays Glob-" and before I can finish, the alarm bells are flashing, "*banker, LIBOR, banker, LIBOR.* . . ." At this point, I want to prostrate myself and moan, "I worked for a bank but I wasn't a . . . a . . . a *banker.*" To date, I have resisted this urge.

This reaction brings me back to CFA Institute; I know it is a highly professional and well-respected organization. I would say that at this time, CFA Institute cannot do too much to encourage the highest standards of ethical behavior in the industry.

I thank you for this award and for the ongoing efforts of the Research Foundation of CFA Institute.

Bibliography

Clarke, R., H. DeSilva, and S. Thorley. 2002. "Portfolio Constraints and the Fundamental Law of Active Management." *Financial Analysts Journal*, vol. 58, no. 5 (September/October):48–66.

Grinold, R. 2007. "Dynamic Portfolio Analysis." *Journal of Portfolio Management*, vol. 34, no. 1 (Fall):12–26.

Grinold, R., and R. Kahn. 2011. "Breadth, Skill and Time." *Journal of Portfolio Management*, vol. 38, no. 1 (Fall):18–28.

Sharpe, W.F. 1991. "The Arithmetic of Active Management." *Financial Analysts Journal*, vol. 47, no. 1 (January/February):7–9.

Treynor, Jack. 2007. *Treynor on Institutional Investing*. Hoboken, NJ: John Wiley & Sons.

Research Foundation Leadership Circle

The Research Foundation Leadership Circle honors investment professionals whose outstanding commitment and contributions have benefited the Research Foundation over an extended period of time. The Research Foundation is honored to recognize the following members of the Leadership Circle:

> Gary Brinson, CFA
>
> George Noyes, CFA
>
> Walter Stern, CFA
>
> James R. Vertin, CFA

Recent Publications from the Research Foundation Archive

2012

Monographs

A New Look at Currency Investing (December)
Momtchil Pojarliev, CFA, and Richard M. Levich

> The authors of this book examine the rationale for investing in currency. They highlight several features of currency returns that make currency an attractive asset class for institutional investors. Using style factors to model currency returns provides a natural way to decompose returns into alpha and beta components. They find that several established currency trading strategies (variants of carry, trend-following, and value strategies) produce consistent returns that can be proxied as style or risk factors and have the nature of beta returns. Then, using two datasets of returns of actual currency hedge funds, they find that some currency managers produce true alpha. Finally, they find that adding to an institutional investor's portfolio even a small amount of currency exposure—particularly to alpha generators—can make a meaningful positive impact on the portfolio's performance.

Life-Cycle Investing: Financial Education and Consumer Protection (November)
Edited by Zvi Bodie, Laurence B. Siegel, and Lisa Stanton, CFA

> Third in the series of Boston University–sponsored conferences titled "The Future of Life-Cycle Saving and Investing," the May 2011 conference again brought together academic researchers, educators, advisers, and regulators. This time, we analyzed the gaps in consumers' current financial knowledge, how those gaps might be narrowed through financial education programs, and how consumer protection regarding financial products might be strengthened—with a focus on low- and middle-income households. Although there was general agreement that consumers of financial products and services make many costly mistakes, there was also considerable disagreement about relying primarily on consumer financial education programs to correct those mistakes.

Fund Management: An Emotional Finance Perspective (August)
David Tuckett and Richard J. Taffler

> To increase understanding of the real world of the fund manager, the authors apply principles from emotional finance. They report their findings from analysing in-depth interviews of 52 traditional and quantitative-oriented equity managers. In particular, they examine the importance of storytelling in the managers' ability to act in the face of uncertainty. The nature of the fund managers' job requires them to cope with emotions that, particularly if denied, can threaten to overwhelm their thinking.

Expected Returns on Major Asset Classes (June)
Antti Ilmanen

> Can the art and science of investment management be reduced to a set of patterns that markets generally follow, in apparent violation of the efficient market hypothesis? Can investors reasonably expect to make money from the knowledge of these patterns, even after they have not only been identified but also widely exploited? Although one's first guess might be that the answers to these questions are no, at least sometimes, the answer is yes.

Literature Reviews

"The New Field of Liquidity and Financial Frictions" (June)
David Adler

> Illiquidity and other financial frictions are critical to financial markets and the overall economy. This literature review provides a synopsis of academic research in this rapidly developing specialty field, offering insights into liquidity and asset pricing, systemic risk, macro frictions, and new models of the causes of a liquidity crisis.

Recent Publications from the Research Foundation Archive

"Equity Valuation and Inflation: A Review" (January)
Stephen E. Wilcox, CFA

> In theory, equity returns should be neutral to inflation. In practice, however, evidence of such behavior in the short run has been difficult to come by. This literature review provides a synopsis of much of the academic and practitioner research regarding the effects of inflation on equity prices.

2011

Monographs

Rethinking the Equity Risk Premium (December)
Edited by P. Brett Hammond, Jr., Martin L. Leibowitz, and Laurence B. Siegel

> In 2001, a small group of academics and practitioners met to discuss the equity risk premium (ERP). Ten years later, in 2011, a similar discussion took place, with participants writing up their thoughts for this volume. The result is a rich set of papers that practitioners may find useful in developing their own approach to the subject.

A Practical Guide to Risk Management (July)
Thomas S. Coleman

> Managing risk is at the core of managing any financial organization. Risk measurement and quantitative tools are critical aids for supporting risk management, but quantitative tools alone are no substitute for judgment, wisdom, and knowledge. Managers within a financial organization must be, before anything else, risk managers in the true sense of managing the risks that the firm faces.

Frontier Market Equity Investing: Finding the Winners of the Future (May)
Lawrence Speidell, CFA

> Frontier markets represent a multitude of distinct cultures and can be overwhelming to investors. The author examines the many opportunities for investing that exist in frontier countries. He reviews the stock markets, the listed companies, the potential returns, and the diversification benefits. He also considers economic and political fundamentals.

A Primer for Investment Trustees (January)
Jeffery V. Bailey, CFA, Jesse L. Phillips, CFA, and Thomas M. Richards, CFA

> This "primer," written as if addressed to a new trustee for a university, is a comprehensive discussion of investment issues relevant not only to investment trustees but also to investment professionals who work with trustees. Taking an individual step-by-step through the process of responsible trusteeship, it offers a solid introduction to basic investment principles.

Literature Reviews

"Commodities as an Investment" (September)
Gerald R. Jensen, CFA, and Jeffrey M. Mercer

> Interest in commodities has grown tremendously, partly because commodities are believed to provide direct exposure to unique factors and have special hedging characteristics. This review discusses the instruments that provide exposure to commodities, the measures and historical record of commodity investment performance, evidence about the benefits of strategic versus tactical commodity allocations, and recent developments in the market.

Recent Publications from the Research Foundation Archive

"Investment Issues in Emerging Markets: A Review" (February)
C. Mitchell Conover, CFA, CIPM

> Emerging markets have generated considerable interest among investors and academics. Although their returns are increasingly converging to those of the developed world because of integration and liberalization, they still provide benefits to a global portfolio. This review reflects the latest practitioner and academic work on emerging market investing.

2010

Monographs

Behavioral Finance and Investment Management (December)
Edited by Arnold S. Wood

> *Behavioral Finance and Investment Management* is a portfolio of different insights by different authors—all intended to help us make better choices. Each piece in some way touches on our biases, our embedded beliefs, and considers how these biases and beliefs can help as well as hinder our decisions. In the beginning, behavioral finance was a loose and easily maligned collection of hypotheses on the scientific frontier. Today, the discipline has achieved respect, and this book gives recognition to a few of the people who have enriched all of us with their research and determination to know what makes us tick.

Investment Management after the Global Financial Crisis (October)
Frank J. Fabozzi, CFA, Sergio M. Focardi, and Caroline Jonas

> The investment industry was severely affected by the global financial crisis of 2007–2009, and changes will have to occur. In this monograph, investment industry players, observers, recruiters, and academics are asked to offer their opinions and ideas about what they think the most profound changes are going to be.

Literature Reviews

"Private Wealth Management: A Review" (July)
William W. Jennings, CFA, Stephen M. Horan, CFA, and William Reichenstein, CFA

> Private wealth management is the investment management specialization focused on high-net-worth individuals and families. Portfolio design and investment solutions in private wealth management are customized to reflect the complexities of the investor's unique circumstances. This review reflects the current best thinking on private wealth management.

RESEARCH FOUNDATION CONTRIBUTION FORM

☑ **Yes**, I want the Research Foundation to continue to fund innovative research that advances the investment management profession. Please accept my tax-deductible contribution at the following level:

    Thought Leadership Circle................. US$1,000,000 or more
    Named Endowment...................... US$100,000 to US$999,999
    Research Fellow .... US$10,000 to US$99,999
    Contributing Donor........................ US$1,000 to US$9,999
    Friend .... Up to US$999

    I would like to donate $ _____.

☐ My check is enclosed (payable to the CFA Institute Research Foundation).
☐ I would like to donate appreciated securities (send me information).
☐ Please charge my donation to my credit card.
    ■ VISA ■ MC ■ Amex ■ Diners ■ Corporate ■ Personal

Card Number

___/___
Expiration Date   Name on card   PLEASE PRINT

☐ Corporate Card
☐ Personal Card
                    Signature

☐ This is a pledge. Please bill me for my donation of $ _____
☐ I would like recognition of my donation to be:
    ■ Individual donation ■ Corporate donation ■ Different individual

_____
PLEASE PRINT NAME OR COMPANY NAME AS YOU WOULD LIKE IT TO APPEAR

PLEASE PRINT ☐ Mr. ☐ Mrs. ☐ Ms. MEMBER NUMBER_____

_____
Last Name (Family Name)   First   Middle Initial

_____
Title

_____
Address

_____
City   State/Province   Country ZIP/Postal Code

**Please mail this completed form with your contribution to:
The CFA Institute Research Foundation • P.O. Box 2082
Charlottesville, VA 22902-2082 USA**

For more on the CFA Institute Research Foundation, please visit www.cfainstitute.org/learning/foundation/.